MW00533831

The
CHOSEN
PRESENTS:

A BLENDED HARMONY OF

THE
Gospels

By
Steve Laube, Amanda Jenkins, and Dallas Jenkins

BroadStreet
PUBLISHING

BroadStreet Publishing® Group, LLC
Savage, Minnesota, USA
BroadStreetPublishing.com

The Chosen Presents: A Blended Harmony of the Gospels
Copyright © 2022 The Chosen, LLC

978-1-4245-6490-3 (faux)
978-1-4245-6491-0 (e-book)

All rights reserved. No part of this book may be reproduced in any form, except for brief quotations in printed reviews, without permission in writing from the publisher.

All Scripture quotations are taken from the Christian Standard Bible®, Copyright © 2017 by Holman Bible Publishers. Used by permission. Christian Standard Bible® and CSB® are federally registered trademarks of Holman Bible Publishers, all rights reserved.

Stock or custom editions of BroadStreet Publishing titles may be purchased in bulk for educational, business, ministry, fundraising, or sales promotional use. For information, please email orders@broadstreetpublishing.com.

Cover and interior by Garborg Design Works | garborgdesign.com

Printed in China

22 23 24 25 26 5 4 3 2 1

Preface by
Dallas and Amanda Jenkins

A number of years ago, we heard a remarkable story from a missionary who worked in Iran. His team was distributing Bibles, but since Christian literature is illegal in that country, the Bibles had to be delivered under cover of darkness out of a secret compartment in the back of a truck.

One night, as the team was en route to a specific location, their car suddenly broke down. While the team tried to ascertain the cause, a stranger approached and in broken English said, "You have Bible."

Fearing the secret police, they hedged.

Again, he said, "You have Bible."

The team hesitated still, uncertain as to how to answer and fearing possible repercussions.

"God told me come," the man continued. "Stand here. Wait for Bible."

Well, in that case—"Yeah. We have Bible."

They gave the man every Bible they had. When he turned to go, the team offered to go with him to preach to the people in the village. But as he disappeared into the darkness, they heard him say, "No. Bible preach."

That story, and those two words, stuck with us. After all, the Bible *is* enough. The message on its pages is everything because it offers new life in Jesus, the long-awaited Savior of the world and the reason we make *The Chosen*.

Which brings us to the book you're holding. As storytellers, we love that this will read like one—a beautiful story that flows and is easy to understand. As lovers of the Bible, we're overjoyed that, unlike the show, every word in this book is "inspired by God and is profitable for teaching, for rebuking, for correcting, for training in righteousness, so that the man [and woman] of God may be complete, equipped for every good work" (2 Timothy 3:16–17, CSB).

We feel blessed to be able to make *The Chosen*, but the truth is that it's just a TV show.

But this…*the Bible* is the reason we do what we do.

In other words, dear reader, Bible preach.

Dallas and Amanda Jenkins

Introduction by Steve Laube

It is an honor and a privilege to work on a project like this. The four Gospels, Matthew, Mark, Luke, and John, are part of the inspired Word of God, given to us as holy Scripture. With differences in style, they were each written to present accurate historical material with a divine purpose. Whoever carefully studies these four accounts eventually forms the larger story in their mind, a blended history of events.

However, it isn't easy to hold the four Gospels in the balance to form that single cohesive narrative. To make matters more difficult, our modern world tells stories chronologically, often with time stamps as a guide, like a documentary. The first-century writers did not think or write in that way. In addition, there are stories found in one Gospel that are not found in others.

To solve this challenge, many scholars over the centuries arranged the words of the four Gospels in parallel columns—*harmonies*. (See the resource section in the back of the book for examples.) There were others who wanted to put the four Gospels into one story instead of in side-by-side columns. Back in AD 160, Tatian, an early church Christian in Syria, wrote his *Diatessaron* where he created a single continuous story from the

Gospels. Other well-known writers, like Augustine and John Calvin, wrote their commentaries in a way to show the Gospels in parallel or connected nature. Following this long-standing practice, we have done something similar, creating a blended harmony of the Gospels.

The goal of this book is to have the Jesus story told in a seamless form. Verse references (originally added to the Bible in 1551) have been removed to avoid having them interfere with the reading. Subheadings are placed before the naturally divided scenes or themes for ease in understanding the flow. In addition, the story is broken into forty readings. This allows the reader to meditate on the life of Jesus each day.

The text of the four Gospels, in their entirety, is the basis of this book without repeating identical parallel sentences. This work is not intended to replace the Scriptures as presented in their original form. In fact, there is an index in the back of the book for each of the sections as an encouragement for the reader to look further into the text itself.

Ultimately, our hope is to encourage you to immerse yourself in the greatest story ever told. Jesus is the center of it all. The apostle John says it so well in his Gospel: These words are "written so that you may believe that Jesus is the Messiah, the Son of God, and that by believing you may have life in his name" (John 20:31, CSB).

Steve Laube

DAY ONE

The Beginning

The beginning of the gospel of Jesus Christ, the Son of God. Many have undertaken to compile a narrative about the events that have been fulfilled among us, just as the original eyewitnesses and servants of the word handed them down to us. So it also seemed good to me, since I have carefully investigated everything from the very first, to write to you in an orderly sequence, most honorable Theophilus, so that you may know the certainty of the things about which you have been instructed.

In the beginning was the Word, and the Word was with God, and the Word was God. He was with God in the beginning. All things were created through him, and apart from him not one thing was created that has been created. In him was life, and that life was the light of men. That light shines in the darkness, and yet the darkness did not overcome it.

There was a man sent from God whose name was John. He came as a witness to testify about the light, so that all might believe through him. He was not the light, but he came to testify about the light. The true light that gives light to everyone was coming into the world.

He was in the world, and the world was created through him, and yet the world did not recognize him. He came to his own, and his own people did not receive him. But to all who did receive him, he gave them the right to be children of God, to those who believe in his name, who were born, not of natural descent, or of the will of the flesh, or of the will of man, but of God.

The Word became flesh and dwelt among us. We observed his glory, the glory as the one and only Son from the Father, full of grace and truth. (John testified concerning him and exclaimed, "This was the one of whom I said, 'The one coming after me ranks ahead of me, because he existed before me.'") Indeed, we have all received grace upon grace from his fullness, for the law was given through Moses; grace and truth came through Jesus Christ. No one has ever seen God. The one and only Son, who is himself God and is at the Father's side—he has revealed him.

The Genealogy from Abraham to Jesus

An account of the genealogy of Jesus Christ, the Son of David, the Son of Abraham:

Abraham fathered Isaac, Isaac fathered Jacob, Jacob fathered Judah and his brothers, Judah fathered Perez and Zerah by Tamar, Perez fathered Hezron, Hezron fathered Aram, Aram fathered Amminadab, Amminadab fathered Nahshon, Nahshon fathered

Salmon, Salmon fathered Boaz by Rahab, Boaz fathered Obed by Ruth, Obed fathered Jesse, and Jesse fathered King David.

David fathered Solomon by Uriah's wife, Solomon fathered Rehoboam, Rehoboam fathered Abijah, Abijah fathered Asa, Asa fathered Jehoshaphat, Jehoshaphat fathered Joram, Joram fathered Uzziah, Uzziah fathered Jotham, Jotham fathered Ahaz, Ahaz fathered Hezekiah, Hezekiah fathered Manasseh, Manasseh fathered Amon, Amon fathered Josiah, and Josiah fathered Jeconiah and his brothers at the time of the exile to Babylon.

After the exile to Babylon Jeconiah fathered Shealtiel, Shealtiel fathered Zerubbabel, Zerubbabel fathered Abiud, Abiud fathered Eliakim, Eliakim fathered Azor, Azor fathered Zadok, Zadok fathered Achim, Achim fathered Eliud, Eliud fathered Eleazar, Eleazar fathered Matthan, Matthan fathered Jacob, and Jacob fathered Joseph the husband of Mary, who gave birth to Jesus who is called the Messiah.

So all the generations from Abraham to David were fourteen generations; and from David until the exile to Babylon, fourteen generations; and from the exile to Babylon until the Messiah, fourteen generations.

The Genealogy from Jesus to Adam

As he began his ministry, Jesus was about thirty years old and was thought to be the son of Joseph, son of

Heli, son of Matthat, son of Levi, son of Melchi, son of Jannai, son of Joseph, son of Mattathias, son of Amos, son of Nahum, son of Esli, son of Naggai, son of Maath, son of Mattathias, son of Semein, son of Josech, son of Joda, son of Joanan, son of Rhesa, son of Zerubbabel, son of Shealtiel, son of Neri, son of Melchi, son of Addi, son of Cosam, son of Elmadam, son of Er, son of Joshua, son of Eliezer, son of Jorim, son of Matthat, son of Levi, son of Simeon, son of Judah, son of Joseph, son of Jonam, son of Eliakim, son of Melea, son of Menna, son of Mattatha, son of Nathan, son of David, son of Jesse, son of Obed, son of Boaz, son of Salmon, son of Nahshon, son of Amminadab, son of Ram, son of Hezron, son of Perez, son of Judah, son of Jacob, son of Isaac, son of Abraham, son of Terah, son of Nahor, son of Serug, son of Reu, son of Peleg, son of Eber, son of Shelah, son of Cainan, son of Arphaxad, son of Shem, son of Noah, son of Lamech, son of Methuselah, son of Enoch, son of Jared, son of Mahalalel, son of Cainan, son of Enos, son of Seth, son of Adam, son of God.

The Birth of John the Baptist Foretold

In the days of King Herod of Judea, there was a priest of Abijah's division named Zechariah. His wife was from the daughters of Aaron, and her name was Elizabeth. Both were righteous in God's sight, living without blame according to all the commands and requirements of the Lord. But they had no children because

DAY ONE ⸺ 11

Elizabeth could not conceive, and both of them were well along in years.

When his division was on duty and he was serving as priest before God, it happened that he was chosen by lot, according to the custom of the priesthood, to enter the sanctuary of the Lord and burn incense. At the hour of incense the whole assembly of the people was praying outside. An angel of the Lord appeared to him, standing to the right of the altar of incense. When Zechariah saw him, he was terrified and overcome with fear. But the angel said to him, "Do not be afraid, Zechariah, because your prayer has been heard. Your wife Elizabeth will bear you a son, and you will name him John. There will be joy and delight for you, and many will rejoice at his birth. For he will be great in the sight of the Lord and will never drink wine or beer. He will be filled with the Holy Spirit while still in his mother's womb. He will turn many of the children of Israel to the Lord their God. And he will go before him in the spirit and power of Elijah, to turn the hearts of fathers to their children, and the disobedient to the understanding of the righteous, to make ready for the Lord a prepared people."

"How can I know this?" Zechariah asked the angel. "For I am an old man, and my wife is well along in years."

The angel answered him, "I am Gabriel, who stands in the presence of God, and I was sent to speak to you and tell you this good news. Now listen. You will become silent and unable to speak until the day these things take place, because you did not believe my words, which will be fulfilled in their proper time."

Meanwhile, the people were waiting for Zechariah, amazed that he stayed so long in the sanctuary. When he did come out, he could not speak to them. Then they realized that he had seen a vision in the sanctuary. He was making signs to them and remained speechless. When the days of his ministry were completed, he went back home.

After these days his wife Elizabeth conceived and kept herself in seclusion for five months. She said, "The Lord has done this for me. He has looked with favor in these days to take away my disgrace among the people."

The Birth of Jesus Revealed to Mary

In the sixth month, the angel Gabriel was sent by God to a town in Galilee called Nazareth, to a virgin engaged to a man named Joseph, of the house of David. The virgin's name was Mary. And the angel came to her and said, "Greetings, favored woman! The Lord is with you." But she was deeply troubled by this statement, wondering what kind of greeting this could be. Then the angel told her, "Do not be afraid, Mary, for you have found favor with God. Now listen: You will conceive and give birth to a son, and you will name him Jesus. He will be great and will be called the Son of the Most High, and the Lord God will give him the throne of his father David. He will reign over the house of Jacob forever, and his kingdom will have no end."

Mary asked the angel, "How can this be, since I have not had sexual relations with a man?"

The angel replied to her, "The Holy Spirit will come upon you, and the power of the Most High will overshadow you. Therefore, the holy one to be born will be called the Son of God. And consider your relative Elizabeth—even she has conceived a son in her old age, and this is the sixth month for her who was called childless. For nothing will be impossible with God."

"See, I am the Lord's servant," said Mary. "May it happen to me as you have said." Then the angel left her.

DAY TWO

Mary Visits Elizabeth

In those days Mary set out and hurried to a town in the hill country of Judah where she entered Zechariah's house and greeted Elizabeth. When Elizabeth heard Mary's greeting, the baby leaped inside her, and Elizabeth was filled with the Holy Spirit. Then she exclaimed with a loud cry, "Blessed are you among women, and your child will be blessed! How could this happen to me, that the mother of my Lord should come to me? For you see, when the sound of your greeting reached my ears, the baby leaped for joy inside me. Blessed is she who has believed that the Lord would fulfill what he has spoken to her!"

Mary's Song of Praise

And Mary said:

> My soul magnifies the Lord,
> and my spirit rejoices in God my Savior,
> because he has looked with favor
> on the humble condition of his servant.
> Surely, from now on all generations

will call me blessed,
because the Mighty One
has done great things for me,
and his name is holy.
His mercy is from generation to generation
on those who fear him.
He has done a mighty deed with his arm;
he has scattered the proud
because of the thoughts of their hearts;
he has toppled the mighty from their thrones
and exalted the lowly.
He has satisfied the hungry with good things
and sent the rich away empty.
He has helped his servant Israel,
remembering his mercy
to Abraham and his descendants forever,
just as he spoke to our ancestors.

And Mary stayed with her about three months; then she returned to her home.

The Birth of John the Baptist

Now the time had come for Elizabeth to give birth, and she had a son. Then her neighbors and relatives heard that the Lord had shown her his great mercy, and they rejoiced with her.

When they came to circumcise the child on the eighth day, they were going to name him Zechariah, after his father. But his mother responded, "No. He will be called John."

Then they said to her, "None of your relatives has that name." So they motioned to his father to find out what he wanted him to be called. He asked for a writing tablet and wrote, "His name is John." And they were all amazed. Immediately his mouth was opened and his tongue set free, and he began to speak, praising God. Fear came on all those who lived around them, and all these things were being talked about throughout the hill country of Judea. All who heard about him took it to heart, saying, "What then will this child become?" For, indeed, the Lord's hand was with him.

The Song of Zechariah

Then his father Zechariah was filled with the Holy Spirit and prophesied:

> Blessed is the Lord, the God of Israel,
> because he has visited
> and provided redemption for his people.
> He has raised up a horn of salvation for us
> in the house of his servant David,
> just as he spoke by the mouth
> of his holy prophets in ancient times;
> salvation from our enemies
> and from the hand of those who hate us.
> He has dealt mercifully with our ancestors
> and remembered his holy covenant—

the oath that he swore to our father Abraham,
to grant that we,
having been rescued
from the hand of our enemies,
would serve him without fear
in holiness and righteousness
in his presence all our days.
And you, child, will be called
a prophet of the Most High,
for you will go before the Lord
to prepare his ways,
to give his people knowledge of salvation
through the forgiveness of their sins.
Because of our God's merciful compassion,
the dawn from on high will visit us
to shine on those who live in darkness
and the shadow of death,
to guide our feet into the way of peace.

The child grew up and became strong in spirit, and he was in the wilderness until the day of his public appearance to Israel.

Joseph Told of Jesus

The birth of Jesus Christ came about this way: After his mother Mary had been engaged to Joseph, it was discovered before they came together that she was pregnant from the Holy Spirit. So her husband, Joseph, being a righteous man, and not wanting to disgrace her publicly, decided to divorce her secretly.

But after he had considered these things, an angel of the Lord appeared to him in a dream, saying, "Joseph, son of David, don't be afraid to take Mary as your wife, because what has been conceived in her is from the Holy Spirit. She will give birth to a son, and you are to name him Jesus, because he will save his people from their sins."

Now all this took place to fulfill what was spoken by the Lord through the prophet:

> See, the virgin will become pregnant
> and give birth to a son,
> and they will name him Immanuel,
>
> which is translated "God is with us."

When Joseph woke up, he did as the Lord's angel had commanded him. He married her but did not have sexual relations with her until she gave birth to a son. And he named him Jesus.

The Birth of Jesus

In those days a decree went out from Caesar Augustus that the whole empire should be registered. This first registration took place while Quirinius was governing Syria. So everyone went to be registered, each to his own town.

Joseph also went up from the town of Nazareth in Galilee, to Judea, to the city of David, which is called

Bethlehem, because he was of the house and family line of David, to be registered along with Mary, who was engaged to him and was pregnant. While they were there, the time came for her to give birth. Then she gave birth to her firstborn son, and she wrapped him tightly in cloth and laid him in a manger, because there was no guest room available for them.

The Shepherds and Angels

In the same region, shepherds were staying out in the fields and keeping watch at night over their flock. Then an angel of the Lord stood before them, and the glory of the Lord shone around them, and they were terrified. But the angel said to them, "Don't be afraid, for look, I proclaim to you good news of great joy that will be for all the people: Today in the city of David a Savior was born for you, who is the Messiah, the Lord. This will be the sign for you: You will find a baby wrapped tightly in cloth and lying in a manger."

Suddenly there was a multitude of the heavenly host with the angel, praising God and saying:

> Glory to God in the highest heaven,
> and peace on earth to people he favors!

When the angels had left them and returned to heaven, the shepherds said to one another, "Let's go straight to Bethlehem and see what has happened, which the Lord has made known to us."

They hurried off and found both Mary and Joseph, and the baby who was lying in the manger. After seeing them, they reported the message they were told about this child, and all who heard it were amazed at what the shepherds said to them. But Mary was treasuring up all these things in her heart and meditating on them. The shepherds returned, glorifying and praising God for all the things they had seen and heard, which were just as they had been told.

The Circumcision and Presentation of Jesus at the Temple

When the eight days were completed for his circumcision, he was named Jesus—the name given by the angel before he was conceived.

And when the days of their purification according to the law of Moses were finished, they brought him up to Jerusalem to present him to the Lord (just as it is written in the law of the Lord, *Every firstborn male will be dedicated to the Lord*) and to offer a sacrifice (according to what is stated in the law of the Lord, *a pair of turtledoves or two young pigeons*).

There was a man in Jerusalem whose name was Simeon. This man was righteous and devout, looking forward to Israel's consolation, and the Holy Spirit was on him. It had been revealed to him by the Holy Spirit that he would not see death before he saw the Lord's Messiah. Guided by the Spirit, he entered the temple. When the parents brought in the child Jesus to perform for him what was customary under the law, Simeon took him up in his arms, praised God, and said,

> Now, Master,
> you can dismiss your servant in peace,
> as you promised.
> For my eyes have seen your salvation.
> You have prepared it
> in the presence of all peoples—
> a light for revelation to the Gentiles
> and glory to your people Israel.

His father and mother were amazed at what was being said about him. Then Simeon blessed them and told his mother Mary, "Indeed, this child is destined to cause the fall and rise of many in Israel and to be a sign that will be opposed—and a sword will pierce your own soul—that the thoughts of many hearts may be revealed."

There was also a prophetess, Anna, a daughter of Phanuel, of the tribe of Asher. She was well along in years, having lived with her husband seven years after her marriage, and was a widow for eighty-four years. She did not leave the temple, serving God night and day with fasting and prayers. At that very moment, she came up and began to thank God and to speak about him to all who were looking forward to the redemption of Jerusalem.

DAY THREE

The Wise Men Visit

After Jesus was born in Bethlehem of Judea in the days of King Herod, wise men from the east arrived in Jerusalem, saying, "Where is he who has been born king of the Jews? For we saw his star at its rising and have come to worship him."

When King Herod heard this, he was deeply disturbed, and all Jerusalem with him. So he assembled all the chief priests and scribes of the people and asked them where the Messiah would be born.

"In Bethlehem of Judea," they told him, "because this is what was written by the prophet:

And you, Bethlehem, in the land of Judah,
are by no means least among the rulers of
Judah:
Because out of you will come a ruler
who will shepherd my people Israel."

Then Herod secretly summoned the wise men and asked them the exact time the star appeared. He sent them to Bethlehem and said, "Go and search carefully for the child. When you find him, report back to me so that I too can go and worship him."

After hearing the king, they went on their way. And there it was—the star they had seen at its rising. It led them until it came and stopped above the place where the child was. When they saw the star, they were overwhelmed with joy. Entering the house, they saw the child with Mary his mother, and falling to their knees, they worshiped him. Then they opened their treasures and presented him with gifts: gold, frankincense, and myrrh. And being warned in a dream not to go back to Herod, they returned to their own country by another route.

Escape to Egypt

After they were gone, an angel of the Lord appeared to Joseph in a dream, saying, "Get up! Take the child and his mother, flee to Egypt, and stay there until I tell you. For Herod is about to search for the child to kill him." So he got up, took the child and his mother during the night, and escaped to Egypt. He stayed there until Herod's death, so that what was spoken by the Lord through the prophet might be fulfilled: *Out of Egypt I called my Son*.

Then Herod, when he realized that he had been outwitted by the wise men, flew into a rage. He gave orders to massacre all the boys in and around Bethlehem who were two years old and under, in keeping with the time he had learned from the wise men.

Then what was spoken through Jeremiah the prophet was fulfilled:

> A voice was heard in Ramah,
> weeping, and great mourning,
> Rachel weeping for her children;
> and she refused to be consoled,
> because they are no more.

Return to Nazareth

After Herod died, an angel of the Lord appeared in a dream to Joseph in Egypt, saying, "Get up, take the child and his mother, and go to the land of Israel, because those who intended to kill the child are dead." So he got up, took the child and his mother, and entered the land of Israel. But when he heard that Archelaus was ruling over Judea in place of his father Herod, he was afraid to go there. And being warned in a dream, he withdrew to the region of Galilee. Then he went and settled in a town called Nazareth to fulfill what was spoken through the prophets, that he would be called a Nazarene.

The Early Years of Jesus

The boy grew up and became strong, filled with wisdom, and God's grace was on him.

Every year his parents traveled to Jerusalem for the Passover Festival. When he was twelve years old, they went up according to the custom of the festival.

After those days were over, as they were returning, the boy Jesus stayed behind in Jerusalem, but his parents did not know it. Assuming he was in the traveling party, they went a day's journey. Then they began looking for him among their relatives and friends. When they did not find him, they returned to Jerusalem to search for him. After three days, they found him in the temple sitting among the teachers, listening to them and asking them questions. And all those who heard him were astounded at his understanding and his answers. When his parents saw him, they were astonished, and his mother said to him, "Son, why have you treated us like this? Your father and I have been anxiously searching for you."

"Why were you searching for me?" he asked them. "Didn't you know that it was necessary for me to be in my Father's house?" But they did not understand what he said to them.

Then he went down with them and came to Nazareth and was obedient to them. His mother kept all these things in her heart. And Jesus increased in wisdom and stature, and in favor with God and with people.

The Ministry of John the Baptist

In the fifteenth year of the reign of Tiberius Caesar, while Pontius Pilate was governor of Judea, Herod was tetrarch of Galilee, his brother Philip tetrarch of the region of Iturea and Trachonitis, and Lysanias tetrarch of Abilene, during the high priesthood of Annas and Caiaphas, God's word came to John the son of Zechariah in the wilderness.

In those days John the Baptist came, preaching in the wilderness of Judea. He went into all the vicinity of the Jordan, proclaiming a baptism of repentance for the forgiveness of sins and saying, "Repent, because the kingdom of heaven has come near!"

As it is written in Isaiah the prophet:

See, I am sending my messenger ahead of you;
he will prepare your way.
A voice of one crying out in the wilderness:
Prepare the way for the Lord;
make his paths straight!

Every valley will be filled,
and every mountain and hill will be made low;
the crooked will become straight,
the rough ways smooth,
and everyone will see the salvation of God

Now John had a camel-hair garment with a leather belt around his waist, and his food was locusts and wild honey. Then people from Jerusalem, all Judea, and all the vicinity of the Jordan were going out to him, and they were baptized by him in the Jordan River, confessing their sins.

He then said to the crowds, many of the Pharisees and Sadducees, who came out to be baptized by him, "Brood of vipers! Who warned you to flee from the coming wrath? Therefore produce fruit consistent with repentance. And don't start saying to yourselves, 'We have Abraham as our father,' for I tell you that God is able to raise up children for Abraham from these stones. The ax is already at the root of the trees. Therefore, every tree that doesn't produce good fruit will be cut down and thrown into the fire."

"What then should we do?" the crowds were asking him.

He replied to them, "The one who has two shirts must share with someone who has none, and the one who has food must do the same."

Tax collectors also came to be baptized, and they asked him, "Teacher, what should we do?"

He told them, "Don't collect any more than what you have been authorized."

Some soldiers also questioned him, "What should we do?"

He said to them, "Don't take money from anyone by force or false accusation, and be satisfied with your wages."

Now the people were waiting expectantly, and all of them were questioning in their hearts whether John might be the Messiah. John answered them all, "I baptize you with water for repentance, but one who is more powerful than I am is coming. I am not worthy to stoop down and untie the strap of his sandals. He will baptize you with the Holy Spirit and fire. His winnowing shovel is in his hand to clear his threshing floor and gather the wheat into his barn, but the chaff he will burn with fire that never goes out." Then, along with many other exhortations, he proclaimed good news to the people.

The Baptism of Jesus

Then Jesus came from Nazareth in Galilee to John at the Jordan, to be baptized by him. But John tried to stop him, saying, "I need to be baptized by you, and yet you come to me?"

Jesus answered him, "Allow it for now, because this is the way for us to fulfill all righteousness." Then John allowed him to be baptized.

When all the people were baptized, Jesus also was baptized. As soon as he came up out of the water, he was praying and saw the heavens being torn open, and the Holy Spirit descended on him in a physical appearance like a dove. And a voice came from heaven: "You are my beloved Son; with you I am well-pleased."

As he began his ministry, Jesus was about thirty years old.

DAY FOUR

The Wilderness Temptation of Jesus

Then Jesus, full of the Holy Spirit, was led immediately by the Spirit into the wilderness to be tempted by the devil. He was with the wild animals. After he had fasted forty days and forty nights, he was hungry. Then the devil approached him and said, "If you are the Son of God, tell these stones to become bread."

Jesus answered, "It is written: 'Man must not live on bread alone but on every word that comes from the mouth of God.'"

Then the devil took him to the holy city, Jerusalem, and had him stand on the pinnacle of the temple, and said to him, "If you are the Son of God, throw yourself down from here. For it is written:

'He will give his angels orders concerning you,
to protect you,
and they will support you with their hands
so that you will not strike
your foot against a stone.'"

Jesus told him, "It is also written: 'Do not test the Lord your God.'"

Again, the devil took him up to a very high mountain and showed him all the kingdoms of the world and their splendor in a moment of time. And he said to him, "I will give you their splendor and all this authority, because it has been given over to me, and I can give it to anyone I want. I will give you all these things if you will fall down and worship me."

Then Jesus told him, "Go away, Satan! For it is written:

'Worship the Lord your God, and serve only him.'"

After the devil had finished every temptation, he departed from him for a time, and angels came and began to serve him.

Who Is John the Baptist?

This was John's testimony when the Jews from Jerusalem sent priests and Levites to ask him, "Who are you?"

He didn't deny it but confessed, "I am not the Messiah."

"What then?" they asked him. "Are you Elijah?"

"I am not," he said.

"Are you the Prophet?"

"No," he answered.

"Who are you, then?" they asked. "We need to give an answer to those who sent us. What can you tell us about yourself?"

He said, "I am a *voice of one crying out in the wilderness: Make straight the way of the Lord*—just as Isaiah the prophet said."

Now they had been sent from the Pharisees. So they asked him, "Why then do you baptize if you aren't the Messiah, or Elijah, or the Prophet?"

"I baptize with water," John answered them. "Someone stands among you, but you don't know him. He is the one coming after me, whose sandal strap I'm not worthy to untie." All this happened in Bethany across the Jordan, where John was baptizing.

John Identifies Jesus as the Son of God

The next day John saw Jesus coming toward him and said, "Look, the Lamb of God, who takes away the sin of the world! This is the one I told you about: 'After me comes a man who ranks ahead of me, because he existed before me.' I didn't know him, but I came baptizing with water so that he might be revealed to Israel." And John testified, "I saw the Spirit descending from heaven like a dove, and he rested on him. I didn't know him, but he who sent me to baptize with water told me, 'The one you see the Spirit descending and resting on—he is the one who baptizes with the Holy Spirit.' I have seen and testified that this is the Son of God."

The First Followers of Jesus

The next day, John was standing with two of his disciples. When he saw Jesus passing by, he said, "Look, the Lamb of God!"

The two disciples heard him say this and followed Jesus. When Jesus turned and noticed them following him, he asked them, "What are you looking for?"

They said to him, "Rabbi" (which means "Teacher"), "where are you staying?"

"Come and you'll see," he replied. So they went and saw where he was staying, and they stayed with him that day. It was about four in the afternoon.

Andrew, Simon Peter's brother, was one of the two who heard John and followed him. He first found his own brother Simon and told him, "We have found the Messiah" (which is translated "the Christ"), and he brought Simon to Jesus.

When Jesus saw him, he said, "You are Simon, son of John. You will be called Cephas" (which is translated "Peter").

The next day Jesus decided to leave for Galilee. He found Philip and told him, "Follow me."

Now Philip was from Bethsaida, the hometown of Andrew and Peter. Philip found Nathanael and told him, "We have found the one Moses wrote about in the law (and so did the prophets): Jesus the son of Joseph, from Nazareth."

"Can anything good come out of Nazareth?" Nathanael asked him.

"Come and see," Philip answered.

Then Jesus saw Nathanael coming toward him and said about him, "Here truly is an Israelite in whom there is no deceit."

"How do you know me?" Nathanael asked.

"Before Philip called you, when you were under the fig tree, I saw you," Jesus answered.

"Rabbi," Nathanael replied, "You are the Son of God; you are the King of Israel!"

Jesus responded to him, "Do you believe because I told you I saw you under the fig tree? You will see greater things than this." Then he said, "Truly I tell you, you will see heaven opened and the angels of God ascending and descending on the Son of Man."

The Wedding at Cana

On the third day a wedding took place in Cana of Galilee. Jesus's mother was there, and Jesus and his disciples were invited to the wedding as well. When the wine ran out, Jesus's mother told him, "They don't have any wine."

"What has this concern of yours to do with me, woman?" Jesus asked. "My hour has not yet come."

"Do whatever he tells you," his mother told the servants.

Now six stone water jars had been set there for Jewish purification. Each contained twenty or thirty gallons.

"Fill the jars with water," Jesus told them. So they filled them to the brim. Then he said to them, "Now draw some out and take it to the headwaiter." And they did.

When the headwaiter tasted the water (after it had become wine), he did not know where it came from—though the servants who had drawn the water knew. He called the groom and told him, "Everyone sets out the fine wine first, then, after people are drunk, the inferior. But you have kept the fine wine until now."

Jesus did this, the first of his signs, in Cana of Galilee. He revealed his glory, and his disciples believed in him.

After this, he went down to Capernaum, together with his mother, his brothers, and his disciples, and they stayed there only a few days.

Jesus at the Temple

The Jewish Passover was near, and so Jesus went up to Jerusalem. In the temple he found people selling oxen, sheep, and doves, and he also found the money changers sitting there. After making a whip out of cords, he drove everyone out of the temple with their sheep and oxen. He also poured out the money changers' coins and overturned the tables. He told those who were selling doves, "Get these things out of here! Stop turning my Father's house into a marketplace!"

And his disciples remembered that it is written: "Zeal for your house will consume me."

So the Jews replied to him, "What sign will you show us for doing these things?"

Jesus answered, "Destroy this temple, and I will raise it up in three days."

Therefore the Jews said, "This temple took forty-six years to build, and will you raise it up in three days?"

But he was speaking about the temple of his body. So when he was raised from the dead, his disciples remembered that he had said this, and they believed the Scripture and the statement Jesus had made.

The Early Reaction to the Miracles of Jesus

While he was in Jerusalem during the Passover Festival, many believed in his name when they saw the signs he was doing. Jesus, however, would not entrust himself to them, since he knew them all and because he did not need anyone to testify about man; for he himself knew what was in man.

DAY
FIVE

Nicodemus Meets with Jesus

There was a man from the Pharisees named Nicodemus, a ruler of the Jews. This man came to him at night and said, "Rabbi, we know that you are a teacher who has come from God, for no one could perform these signs you do unless God were with him."

Jesus replied, "Truly I tell you, unless someone is born again, he cannot see the kingdom of God."

"How can anyone be born when he is old?" Nicodemus asked him. "Can he enter his mother's womb a second time and be born?"

Jesus answered, "Truly I tell you, unless someone is born of water and the Spirit, he cannot enter the kingdom of God. Whatever is born of the flesh is flesh, and whatever is born of the Spirit is spirit. Do not be amazed that I told you that you must be born again. The wind blows where it pleases, and you hear its sound, but you don't know where it comes from or where it is going. So it is with everyone born of the Spirit."

"How can these things be?" asked Nicodemus.

"Are you a teacher of Israel and don't know these things?" Jesus replied. "Truly I tell you, we speak what we know and we testify to what we have seen, but you do not accept our testimony. If I have told you about earthly things and you don't believe, how will you believe if I tell you about heavenly things? No one has ascended into heaven except the one who descended from heaven —the Son of Man.

"Just as Moses lifted up the snake in the wilderness, so the Son of Man must be lifted up, so that everyone who believes in him may have eternal life. For God loved the world in this way: He gave his one and only Son, so that everyone who believes in him will not perish but have eternal life. For God did not send his Son into the world to condemn the world, but to save the world through him. Anyone who believes in him is not condemned, but anyone who does not believe is already condemned, because he has not believed in the name of the one and only Son of God. This is the judgment: The light has come into the world, and people loved darkness rather than the light because their deeds were evil. For everyone who does evil hates the light and avoids it, so that his deeds may not be exposed. But anyone who lives by the truth comes to the light, so that his works may be shown to be accomplished by God."

John the Baptist Points to Jesus

After this, Jesus and his disciples went to the Judean countryside, where he spent time with them and baptized.

John also was baptizing in Aenon near Salim, because there was plenty of water there. People were coming and being baptized, since John had not yet been thrown into prison.

Then a dispute arose between John's disciples and a Jew about purification. So they came to John and told him, "Rabbi, the one you testified about, and who was with you across the Jordan, is baptizing—and everyone is going to him."

John responded, "No one can receive anything unless it has been given to him from heaven. You yourselves can testify that I said, 'I am not the Messiah, but I've been sent ahead of him.' He who has the bride is the groom. But the groom's friend, who stands by and listens for him, rejoices greatly at the groom's voice. So this joy of mine is complete. He must increase, but I must decrease."

The one who comes from above is above all. The one who is from the earth is earthly and speaks in earthly terms. The one who comes from heaven is above all. He testifies to what he has seen and heard, and yet no one accepts his testimony. The one who has accepted his testimony has affirmed that God is true. For the one whom God sent speaks God's words, since he gives the Spirit without measure. The Father loves the Son and has given all things into his hands. The one who believes in the Son has eternal life, but the one who rejects the Son will not see life; instead, the wrath of God remains on him.

Jesus Travels from Judea through Samaria

But when John rebuked Herod the tetrarch because of Herodias, his brother's wife, and all the evil things he had done, Herod added this to everything else—he locked up John in prison.

Jesus returned to Galilee in the power of the Spirit when he heard that John had been arrested.

When Jesus learned that the Pharisees had heard he was making and baptizing more disciples than John (though Jesus himself was not baptizing, but his disciples were), he left Judea and went again to Galilee. He had to travel through Samaria.

Jesus and the Samaritan Woman at the Well

So he came to a town of Samaria called Sychar near the property that Jacob had given his son Joseph. Jacob's well was there, and Jesus, worn out from his journey, sat down at the well. It was about noon.

A woman of Samaria came to draw water.

"Give me a drink," Jesus said to her, because his disciples had gone into town to buy food.

"How is it that you, a Jew, ask for a drink from me, a Samaritan woman?" she asked him. For Jews do not associate with Samaritans.

Jesus answered, "If you knew the gift of God, and who is saying to you, 'Give me a drink,' you would ask him, and he would give you living water."

"Sir," said the woman, "you don't even have a bucket, and the well is deep. So where do you get this 'living water'? You aren't greater than our father Jacob, are you? He gave us the well and drank from it himself, as did his sons and livestock."

Jesus said, "Everyone who drinks from this water will get thirsty again. But whoever drinks from the water that I will give him will never get thirsty again. In fact, the water I will give him will become a well of water springing up in him for eternal life."

"Sir," the woman said to him, "give me this water so that I won't get thirsty and come here to draw water."

"Go call your husband," he told her, "and come back here."

"I don't have a husband," she answered.

"You have correctly said, 'I don't have a husband,'" Jesus said. "For you've had five husbands, and the man you now have is not your husband. What you have said is true."

"Sir," the woman replied, "I see that you are a prophet. Our ancestors worshiped on this mountain, but you Jews say that the place to worship is in Jerusalem."

Jesus told her, "Believe me, woman, an hour is coming when you will worship the Father neither on this mountain nor in Jerusalem. You Samaritans worship what you do not know. We worship what we do know, because salvation is from the Jews. But an hour is coming, and is now here, when the true worshipers will worship the Father in Spirit and in truth. Yes, the Father wants such people to worship him. God is spirit, and those who worship him must worship in Spirit and in truth."

The woman said to him, "I know that the Messiah is coming" (who is called Christ). "When he comes, he will explain everything to us."

Jesus told her, "I, the one speaking to you, am he."

A Spiritual Harvest

Just then his disciples arrived, and they were amazed that he was talking with a woman. Yet no one said, "What do you want?" or "Why are you talking with her?"

Then the woman left her water jar, went into town, and told the people, "Come, see a man who told me everything I ever did. Could this be the Messiah?" They left the town and made their way to him.

In the meantime the disciples kept urging him, "Rabbi, eat something."

But he said, "I have food to eat that you don't know about."

The disciples said to one another, "Could someone have brought him something to eat?"

"My food is to do the will of him who sent me and to finish his work," Jesus told them. "Don't you say, 'There are still four more months, and then comes the harvest'? Listen to what I'm telling you: Open your eyes and look at the fields, because they are ready for harvest. The reaper is already receiving pay and gathering fruit for eternal life, so that the sower and reaper can rejoice together. For in this case the saying is true: 'One sows and another reaps.' I sent you to reap what you didn't labor for; others have labored, and you have benefited from their labor."

Now many Samaritans from that town believed in him because of what the woman said when she testified, "He told me everything I ever did." So when the Samaritans came to him, they asked him to stay with them, and he stayed there two days. Many more believed because of what he said. And they told the woman, "We no longer believe because of what you said, since we have heard for ourselves and know that this really is the Savior of the world."

DAY
SIX

Jesus Returns to Galilee

After two days he left there for Galilee. (Jesus himself had testified that a prophet has no honor in his own country.) When they entered Galilee, the Galileans welcomed him because they had seen everything he did in Jerusalem during the festival. For they also had gone to the festival.

From then on Jesus began to preach, proclaiming the good news of God, "The time is fulfilled, and the kingdom of God has come near. Repent and believe the good news!"

News about him spread throughout the entire vicinity. He was teaching in their synagogues, being praised by everyone.

Jesus Heals an Official's Son

He went again to Cana of Galilee, where he had turned the water into wine. There was a certain royal official whose son was ill at Capernaum. When this man heard that Jesus had come from Judea into Galilee, he went to him and pleaded with him to come down and heal his son, since he was about to die.

Jesus told him, "Unless you people see signs and wonders, you will not believe."

"Sir," the official said to him, "come down before my boy dies."

"Go," Jesus told him, "your son will live." The man believed what Jesus said to him and departed.

While he was still going down, his servants met him saying that his boy was alive. He asked them at what time he got better. "Yesterday at one in the afternoon the fever left him," they answered. The father realized this was the very hour at which Jesus had told him, "Your son will live." So he himself believed, along with his whole household.

Now this was also the second sign Jesus performed after he came from Judea to Galilee.

Jesus Rejected at Nazareth

He came to Nazareth, where he had been brought up. As usual, he entered the synagogue on the Sabbath day and stood up to read. The scroll of the prophet Isaiah was given to him, and unrolling the scroll, he found the place where it was written:

> The Spirit of the Lord is on me,
> because he has anointed me
> to preach good news to the poor.
> He has sent me

to proclaim release to the captives
and recovery of sight to the blind,
to set free the oppressed,
to proclaim the year of the Lord's favor.

He then rolled up the scroll, gave it back to the attendant, and sat down. And the eyes of everyone in the synagogue were fixed on him. He began by saying to them, "Today as you listen, this Scripture has been fulfilled."

They were all speaking well of him and were amazed by the gracious words that came from his mouth; yet they said, "Isn't this Joseph's son?"

Then he said to them, "No doubt you will quote this proverb to me: 'Doctor, heal yourself. What we've heard that took place in Capernaum, do here in your hometown also.'"

He also said, "Truly I tell you, no prophet is accepted in his hometown. But I say to you, there were certainly many widows in Israel in Elijah's days, when the sky was shut up for three years and six months while a great famine came over all the land. Yet Elijah was not sent to any of them except a widow at Zarephath in Sidon. And in the prophet Elisha's time, there were many in Israel who had leprosy, and yet not one of them was cleansed except Naaman the Syrian."

When they heard this, everyone in the synagogue was enraged. They got up, drove him out of town, and brought him to the edge of the hill that their town was built on, intending to hurl him over the cliff. But he passed right through the crowd and went on his way.

Jesus Moves to Capernaum

He left Nazareth and went to live in Capernaum by the sea, in the region of Zebulun and Naphtali. This was to fulfill what was spoken through the prophet Isaiah:

> Land of Zebulun and land of Naphtali,
> along the road by the sea, beyond the Jordan,
> Galilee of the Gentiles.
> The people who live in darkness
> have seen a great light,
> and for those living in the land
> of the shadow of death,
> a light has dawned.

Jesus Calls Four Fisherman

As Jesus was walking along the Sea of Galilee, with the crowd pressing in to hear God's word, he saw two brothers, Simon (who is called Peter), and his brother Andrew. They were casting a net into the sea—for they were fishermen. He saw two boats at the edge of the lake; the fishermen had left them and were washing their nets. He got into one of the boats, which belonged to Simon, and asked him to put out a little from the land. Then he sat down and was teaching the crowds from the boat.

When he had finished speaking, he said to Simon, "Put out into deep water and let down your nets for a catch."

"Master," Simon replied, "we've worked hard all night long and caught nothing. But if you say so, I'll let down the nets."

When they did this, they caught a great number of fish, and their nets began to tear. So they signaled to their partners in the other boat to come and help them; they came and filled both boats so full that they began to sink.

When Simon Peter saw this, he fell at Jesus's knees and said, "Go away from me, because I'm a sinful man, Lord!" For he and all those with him were amazed at the catch of fish they had taken, and so were James and John, Zebedee's sons, who were Simon's partners.

"Don't be afraid," Jesus told Simon. "From now on you will be catching people." Then immediately they brought the boats to land, left everything, and followed him.

The other brothers, James the son of Zebedee, and his brother John, were in a boat with Zebedee their father, preparing their nets, and he called them. Immediately they left their father in the boat with the hired men and followed him.

Jesus Confronts a Demonized Man

They went into Capernaum, and right away he entered the synagogue on the Sabbath and began to teach. They were astonished at his teaching because he was teaching them as one who had authority, and not like the scribes.

In the synagogue there was a man with an unclean demonic spirit who cried out with a loud voice, "Leave us alone! What do you have to do with us, Jesus of Nazareth? Have you come to destroy us? I know who you are—the Holy One of God!"

But Jesus rebuked him and said, "Be silent and come out of him!" And throwing him down before them and threw him into convulsions, the demon shouted with a loud voice and came out of him without hurting him at all.

They were all amazed, and so they began to ask each other, "What is this message? A new teaching with authority and power! He commands even the unclean spirits, and they obey him." At once the news about him spread throughout the entire vicinity of Galilee.

Jesus Heals Peter's Mother-in-Law

As soon as they left the synagogue, they went into Simon and Andrew's house with James and John. Simon's mother-in-law was lying in bed with a fever, and they told him about her at once. So he went to her, took her by the hand, and raised her up. The fever left her, and she began to serve them.

When the sun was setting, all those who had anyone sick with various diseases brought them to him. As he laid his hands on each one of them, he healed them. Also, he drove out the spirits with a word, and demons were coming out of many, shouting and saying, "You are the Son of God!" But he rebuked them and would not allow them to speak, because they knew he was the Messiah.

This was so that what was spoken through the prophet Isaiah might be fulfilled:

> He himself took our weaknesses
> and carried our diseases.

DAY SEVEN

Jesus Preaches in Galilee

Very early in the morning, while it was still dark, Jesus got up, went out, and made his way to a deserted place; and there he was praying. Simon and his companions searched for him, and when they found him they said, "Everyone is looking for you."

But the crowds were searching for him. They came to him and tried to keep him from leaving them. But he said to them, "It is necessary for me to proclaim the good news about the kingdom of God to the other towns also, because I was sent for this purpose."

Jesus began to go all over Galilee, teaching in their synagogues, preaching the good news of the kingdom, and healing every disease and sickness among the people and driving out demons. Then the news about him spread throughout Syria. So they brought to him all those who were afflicted, those suffering from various diseases and intense pains, the demon-possessed, the epileptics, and the paralytics. And he healed them. Large crowds followed him from Galilee, the Decapolis, Jerusalem, Judea, and beyond the Jordan.

Jesus Heals a Leper

While he was in one of the towns, a man was there who had leprosy all over him. He saw Jesus, fell on his knees facedown, and begged him, "Lord, if you are willing, you can make me clean."

Moved with compassion, Jesus reached out his hand and touched him. "I am willing," he told him. "Be made clean." Immediately the leprosy left him, and he was made clean.

Then Jesus sternly warned him and sent him away at once, telling him, "See that you say nothing to anyone; but go and show yourself to the priest, and offer what Moses commanded for your cleansing, as a testimony to them." Yet he went out and began to proclaim it widely and to spread the news, with the result that Jesus could no longer enter a town openly. But he was out in deserted places, and they came to him from everywhere to hear him and to be healed of their sicknesses. Yet he often withdrew to deserted places and prayed.

Jesus Heals a Paralytic

When he entered Capernaum again after some days, it was reported that he was at home. So many people gathered together that there was no more room, not even in the doorway, and he was speaking the word to them.

Pharisees and teachers of the law were sitting there who had come from every village of Galilee and Judea, and also from Jerusalem. And the Lord's power to heal was in him. Just then four men came, carrying on a stretcher a man who was paralyzed. They tried to bring him in and set him down before him. Since they could not find a way to bring him in because of the crowd, they went up on the roof, removed the roof above him, and after digging through it, lowered him on the stretcher through the roof tiles into the middle of the crowd before Jesus.

Seeing their faith he said, "Friend, have courage, son, your sins are forgiven."

Then the scribes and the Pharisees began to think to themselves, "Who is this man who speaks blasphemies? Who can forgive sins but God alone?"

Right away Jesus perceived in his spirit that they were thinking like this within themselves and said to them, "Why are you thinking these evil things in your hearts? Which is easier: to say to the paralytic, 'Your sins are forgiven,' or to say, 'Get up, take your mat, and walk'? But so that you may know that the Son of Man has authority on earth to forgive sins"—he told the paralytic—"I tell you: get up, take your stretcher, and go home."

Immediately he got up before them, picked up what he had been lying on, and went home glorifying God. Then everyone was astounded, and they were giving glory to God who had given such authority to men. And they were filled with awe and said, "We have seen incredible things today."

The Calling of a Tax Collector

Jesus went out again beside the sea. The whole crowd was coming to him, and he was teaching them. Then, passing by, he saw Matthew, the son of Alphaeus sitting at the tax office, and he said to him, "Follow me." So, leaving everything behind, he got up and began to follow him.

Then Matthew hosted a grand banquet for him at his house. Now there was a large crowd of tax collectors and sinners who were reclining at the table with Jesus and the disciples, for there were many who were following him. But the Pharisees and their scribes were complaining to his disciples, "Why do you eat and drink with tax collectors and sinners?"

When Jesus heard this, he told them, "It is not those who are well who need a doctor, but those who are sick. Go and learn what this means: 'I desire mercy and not sacrifice.' For I didn't come to call the righteous, but sinners."

The Parable of Wineskins

Now John's disciples and the Pharisees were fasting. John's disciples came and asked Jesus, "Why do John's disciples and the Pharisees' disciples often fast and pray, but your disciples do not fast? Yours eat and drink."

Jesus said to them, "The wedding guests cannot fast while the groom is with them, can they? As long as they have the groom with them, they cannot fast. But the time will come when the groom will be taken away from them, and then they will fast on that day."

He also told them a parable: "No one tears a patch from a new garment and puts it on an old garment. Otherwise, not only will he tear the new, because the patch pulls away from the garment and makes the tear worse, but also the piece from the new garment will not match the old. And no one puts new wine into old wineskins. Otherwise, the new wine will burst the skins, it will spill, and the skins will be ruined. No, new wine is put into fresh wineskins. And no one, after drinking old wine, wants new, because he says, 'The old is better.'"

Jesus Heals on the Sabbath

After this, a Jewish festival took place, and Jesus went up to Jerusalem. By the Sheep Gate in Jerusalem there is a pool, called Bethesda in Aramaic, which has five colonnades. Within these lay a large number of the disabled—blind, lame, and paralyzed.

One man was there who had been disabled for thirty-eight years. When Jesus saw him lying there and realized he had already been there a long time, he said to him, "Do you want to get well?"

"Sir," the disabled man answered, "I have no one to put me into the pool when the water is stirred up, but while I'm coming, someone goes down ahead of me."

"Get up," Jesus told him, "pick up your mat and walk." Instantly the man got well, picked up his mat, and started to walk.

Now that day was the Sabbath, and so the Jews said to the man who had been healed, "This is the Sabbath. The law prohibits you from picking up your mat."

He replied, "The man who made me well told me, 'Pick up your mat and walk.'"

DAY EIGHT

Jesus Defends His Sabbath Healings

"Who is this man who told you, 'Pick up your mat and walk'?" they asked. But the man who was healed did not know who it was, because Jesus had slipped away into the crowd that was there.

After this, Jesus found him in the temple and said to him, "See, you are well. Do not sin anymore, so that something worse doesn't happen to you." The man went and reported to the Jews that it was Jesus who had made him well. Therefore, the Jews began persecuting Jesus because he was doing these things on the Sabbath.

Jesus responded to them, "My Father is still working, and I am working also." This is why the Jews began trying all the more to kill him: Not only was he breaking the Sabbath, but he was even calling God his own Father, making himself equal to God.

Jesus replied, "Truly I tell you, the Son is not able to do anything on his own, but only what he sees the Father doing. For whatever the Father does, the Son likewise does these things. For the Father loves the Son and shows him everything he is doing, and he will show him greater works than these so that you will be amazed. And just as the Father raises the dead and gives them life, so the Son also gives life to whom he wants. The Father, in fact, judges no one but has given all judgment to the Son, so that all people may honor the Son just as they honor the Father. Anyone who does not honor the Son does not honor the Father who sent him.

"Truly I tell you, anyone who hears my word and believes him who sent me has eternal life and will not come under judgment but has passed from death to life.

"Truly I tell you, an hour is coming, and is now here, when the dead will hear the voice of the Son of God, and those who hear will live. For just as the Father has life in himself, so also he has granted to the Son to have life in himself. And he has granted him the right to pass judgment, because he is the Son of Man. Do not be amazed at this, because a time is coming when all who are in the graves will hear his voice and come out—those who have done good things, to the resurrection of life, but those who have done wicked things, to the resurrection of condemnation.

"I can do nothing on my own. I judge only as I hear, and my judgment is just, because I do not seek my own will, but the will of him who sent me.

"If I testify about myself, my testimony is not true. There is another who testifies about me, and I know that the testimony he gives about me is true. You sent messengers to John, and he testified to the truth.

I don't receive human testimony, but I say these things so that you may be saved. John was a burning and shining lamp, and you were willing to rejoice for a while in his light.

"But I have a greater testimony than John's because of the works that the Father has given me to accomplish. These very works I am doing testify about me that the Father has sent me. The Father who sent me has himself testified about me. You have not heard his voice at any time, and you haven't seen his form. You don't have his word residing in you, because you don't believe the one he sent. You pore over the Scriptures because you think you have eternal life in them, and yet they testify about me. But you are not willing to come to me so that you may have life.

"I do not accept glory from people, but I know you—that you have no love for God within you. I have come in my Father's name, and yet you don't accept me. If someone else comes in his own name, you will accept him. How can you believe, since you accept glory from one another but don't seek the glory that comes from the only God? Do not think that I will accuse you to the Father. Your accuser is Moses, on whom you have set your hope. For if you believed Moses, you would believe me, because he wrote about me. But if you don't believe what he wrote, how will you believe my words?"

More Sabbath Controversy

On a Sabbath, he passed through the grainfields. His disciples were picking heads of grain, rubbing them in their hands, and eating them. But some of the Pharisees said, "Why are you doing what is not lawful on the Sabbath?"

He said to them, "Have you never read what David and those who were with him did when he was in need and hungry—how he entered the house of God in the time of Abiathar the high priest and ate the bread of the Presence—which is not lawful for anyone to eat except the priests—and also gave some to his companions? Or haven't you read in the law that on Sabbath days the priests in the temple violate the Sabbath and are innocent? I tell you that something greater than the temple is here."

"If you had known what this means, 'I desire mercy and not sacrifice,' you would not have condemned the innocent." Then he told them, "The Sabbath was made for man and not man for the Sabbath. So then, the Son of Man is Lord even of the Sabbath."

On another Sabbath he entered the synagogue and was teaching. A man was there whose right hand was shriveled. The scribes and Pharisees were watching him closely, to see if he would heal on the Sabbath, so that they could find a charge against him. In order to accuse him they asked him, "Is it lawful to heal on the Sabbath?" But he knew their thoughts and told the man with the shriveled hand, "Get up and stand here." So he got up and stood there.

Then he said to them, "Is it lawful to do good on the Sabbath or to do evil, to save life or to kill?" But they were silent. After looking around at them with anger, he was grieved at the hardness of their hearts. He replied to them, "Who among you, if he had a sheep that fell into a pit on the Sabbath, wouldn't take hold of it and lift it out? A person is worth far more than a sheep; so it is lawful to do what is good on the Sabbath."

Then he told the man, "Stretch out your hand." So he stretched it out, and it was restored, as good as the other. Immediately the Pharisees went out filled with rage and started plotting with the Herodians against him, how they might kill him.

Jesus Withdraws and the Crowds Follow

Jesus was aware of this and departed with his disciples to the sea, and a large crowd followed from Galilee, and a large crowd followed from Judea, Jerusalem, Idumea, beyond the Jordan, and around Tyre and Sidon. The large crowd came to him because they heard about everything he was doing. Then he told his disciples to have a small boat ready for him, so that the crowd wouldn't crush him. Since he had healed many, all who had diseases were pressing toward him to touch him. Whenever the unclean spirits saw him, they fell down before him and cried out, "You are the Son of God!" And he would strongly warn them not to make him known so that what was spoken through the prophet Isaiah might be fulfilled:

> Here is my servant whom I have chosen,
> my beloved in whom I delight;
> I will put my Spirit on him,
> and he will proclaim justice to the nations.
> He will not argue or shout,
> and no one will hear his voice in the streets.
> He will not break a bruised reed,
> and he will not put out a smoldering wick,
> until he has led justice to victory.
> The nations will put their hope in his name.

Jesus Appoints His Twelve Apostles

During those days he went out to the mountain to pray and spent all night in prayer to God. When daylight came, he summoned his disciples, and he chose twelve of them, whom he also named apostles to be with him, to send them out to preach, and to have authority to drive out demons.

He appointed the Twelve: To Simon, he gave the name Peter; and to James the son of Zebedee, and to his brother John, he gave the name "Boanerges" (that is, "Sons of Thunder"); Andrew; Philip and Bartholomew; Matthew and Thomas; James the son of Alphaeus, and Thaddaeus; Simon the Zealot, and Judas Iscariot, who also betrayed him.

The Sermon on the Mount

When he saw the crowds, he went up on the mountain, and after he sat down, his disciples came to him. Then he began to teach them, saying:

The Blessings and Woes of the Kingdom

> "Blessed are the poor in spirit,
>   for the kingdom of heaven is theirs.
> Blessed are those who mourn,
>   for they will be comforted.
> Blessed are the humble,
>   for they will inherit the earth.
> Blessed are those who hunger and thirst for righteousness,
>   for they will be filled.
>
> Blessed are the merciful,
>   for they will be shown mercy.
> Blessed are the pure in heart,
>   for they will see God.
> Blessed are the peacemakers,
>   for they will be called sons of God.

Blessed are those who are persecuted because of righteousness,
> for the kingdom of heaven is theirs.

Blessed are you who are hungry now,
> because you will be filled.

Blessed are you who weep now,
> because you will laugh.

Blessed are you when people hate you,
> when they exclude you, insult you,
> and slander your name as evil
> because of the Son of Man.

Rejoice in that day and leap for joy. Take note—your reward is great in heaven, for this is the way their ancestors used to treat the prophets.

But woe to you who are rich,
> for you have received your comfort.

Woe to you who are now full,
> for you will be hungry.

Woe to you who are now laughing,
> for you will mourn and weep.

Woe to you when all people speak well of you,
> for this is the way their ancestors
> used to treat the false prophets."

Salt and Light

"You are the salt of the earth. But if the salt should lose its taste, how can it be made salty? It's no longer good for anything but to be thrown out and trampled under people's feet.

"You are the light of the world. A city situated on a hill cannot be hidden. No one lights a lamp and puts it under a basket, but rather on a lampstand, and it gives light for all who are in the house. In the same way, let your light shine before others, so that they may see your good works and give glory to your Father in heaven.

"Don't think that I came to abolish the Law or the Prophets. I did not come to abolish but to fulfill. For truly I tell you, until heaven and earth pass away, not the smallest letter or one stroke of a letter will pass away from the law until all things are accomplished. Therefore, whoever breaks one of the least of these commands and teaches others to do the same will be called least in the kingdom of heaven. But whoever does and teaches these commands will be called great in the kingdom of heaven. For I tell you, unless your righteousness surpasses that of the scribes and Pharisees, you will never get into the kingdom of heaven."

A New Way of Thinking

"You have heard that it was said to our ancestors, 'Do not murder,' and whoever murders will be subject to judgment. But I tell you, everyone who is angry with his brother or sister will be subject to judgment. Whoever insults his brother or sister, will be subject to the court. Whoever says, 'You fool!' will be subject to hellfire. So if you are offering your gift on the altar, and there you remember that your brother or sister has something against you, leave your gift there in front of the altar. First go and be reconciled with your brother or sister, and then come and offer your gift. Reach a settlement quickly with your adversary while you're on the way with him to the court, or your adversary will hand you over to the judge, and the judge to the officer, and you will be thrown into prison. Truly I tell you, you will never get out of there until you have paid the last penny.

"You have heard that it was said, 'Do not commit adultery.' But I tell you, everyone who looks at a woman lustfully has already committed adultery with her in his heart. If your right eye causes you to sin, gouge it out and throw it away. For it is better that you lose one of the parts of your body than for your whole body to be thrown into hell. And if your right hand causes you to sin, cut it off and throw it away. For it is better that you lose one of the parts of your body than for your whole body to go into hell.

"It was also said, 'Whoever divorces his wife must give her a written notice of divorce.' But I tell you, everyone who divorces his wife, except in a case of sexual immorality, causes her to commit adultery. And whoever marries a divorced woman commits adultery.

"Again, you have heard that it was said to our ancestors, 'You must not break your oath, but you must keep your oaths to the Lord.' But I tell you, don't take an oath at all: either by heaven, because it is God's throne; or by the earth, because it is his footstool; or by Jerusalem, because it is the city of the great King. Do not swear by your head, because you cannot make a single hair white or black. But let your 'yes' mean 'yes,' and your 'no' mean 'no.' Anything more than this is from the evil one.

"You have heard that it was said, 'An eye for an eye' and 'a tooth for a tooth.' But I tell you, don't resist an evildoer. On the contrary, if anyone slaps you on your right cheek, turn the other to him also. As for the one who wants to sue you and take away your shirt, let him have your coat as well. And if anyone forces you to go one mile, go with him two. Give to the one who asks you, and don't turn away from the one who wants to borrow from you.

"You have heard that it was said, 'Love your neighbor' and 'hate your enemy.' But I tell you, love your enemies and pray for those who persecute you, so that you may be children of your Father in heaven. For he causes his sun to rise on the evil and the good, and sends rain on the righteous and the unrighteous. For if you love those who love you, what reward will you have? Don't even the tax collectors do the same? And if you greet only your brothers and sisters, what are you doing out of the ordinary? Don't even the Gentiles do the same? And if you lend to those from whom you expect to receive, what credit is that to you? Even sinners lend to sinners to be repaid in full. But love your enemies, do what is good, and lend, expecting nothing in return. Then your reward will be great, and you will be children of the Most High. For he is gracious to the ungrateful and evil.

"Be merciful, just as your Father also is merciful. Be perfect, therefore, as your heavenly Father is perfect.

"Be careful not to practice your righteousness in front of others to be seen by them. Otherwise, you have no reward with your Father in heaven. So whenever you give to the poor, don't sound a trumpet before you, as the hypocrites do in the synagogues and on the streets, to be applauded by people. Truly I tell you, they have their reward. But when you give to the poor, don't let your left hand know what your right hand is doing, so that your giving may be in secret. And your Father who sees in secret will reward you."

How to Pray

"Whenever you pray, you must not be like the hypocrites, because they love to pray standing in the synagogues and on the street corners to be seen by people. Truly I tell you, they have their reward. But when you pray, go into your private room, shut your door, and pray to your Father who is in secret. And your Father who sees in secret will reward you. When you pray, don't babble like the Gentiles, since they imagine they'll be heard for their many words. Don't be like them, because your Father knows the things you need before you ask him.

"Therefore, you should pray like this:

Our Father in heaven,
    your name be honored as holy.
Your kingdom come.
Your will be done
    on earth as it is in heaven.
Give us today our daily bread.
And forgive us our debts,
    as we also have forgiven our debtors.
And do not bring us into temptation,
    but deliver us from the evil one.

"For if you forgive others their offenses, your heavenly Father will forgive you as well. But if you don't forgive others, your Father will not forgive your offenses.

"Whenever you fast, don't be gloomy like the hypocrites. For they disfigure their faces so that their fasting is obvious to people. Truly I tell you, they have their reward. But when you fast, put oil on your head and wash your face, so that your fasting isn't obvious to others but to your Father who is in secret. And your Father who sees in secret will reward you."

Store Your Treasures in Heaven

"Don't store up for yourselves treasures on earth, where moth and rust destroy and where thieves break in and steal. But store up for yourselves treasures in heaven, where neither moth nor rust destroys, and where thieves don't break in and steal. For where your treasure is, there your heart will be also.

"The eye is the lamp of the body. If your eye is healthy, your whole body will be full of light. But if your eye is bad, your whole body will be full of darkness. So if the light within you is darkness, how deep is that darkness!

"No one can serve two masters, since either he will hate one and love the other, or he will be devoted to one and despise the other. You cannot serve both God and money."

God Will Provide

"Therefore I tell you: Don't worry about your life, what you will eat or what you will drink; or about your body, what you will wear. Isn't life more than food and the body more than clothing? Consider the birds of the sky: They don't sow or reap or gather into barns, yet your heavenly Father feeds them. Aren't you worth more than they? Can any of you add one moment to his life span by worrying? And why do you worry about clothes? Observe how the wildflowers of the field grow: They don't labor or spin thread. Yet I tell you that not even Solomon in all his splendor was adorned like one of these. If that's how God clothes the grass of the field, which is here today and thrown into the furnace tomorrow, won't he do much more for you— you of little faith? So don't worry, saying, 'What will we eat?' or 'What will we drink?' or 'What will we wear?' For the Gentiles eagerly seek all these things, and your heavenly Father knows that you need them. But seek first the kingdom of God and his righteousness, and all these things will be provided for you. Therefore don't worry about tomorrow, because tomorrow will worry about itself. Each day has enough trouble of its own."

Seek Humility and Wisdom

"Do not judge, so that you won't be judged. Do not condemn, and you will not be condemned. Forgive, and you will be forgiven. Give, and it will be given to you; a good measure—pressed down, shaken together, and running over—will be poured into your lap. For you will be judged by the same standard with which you judge others, and you will be measured by the same measure you use. Why do you look at the splinter in your brother's eye but don't notice the beam of wood in your own eye? Or how can you say to your brother, 'Let me take the splinter out of your eye,' and look, there's a beam of wood in your own eye? Hypocrite! First take the beam of wood out of your eye, and then you will see clearly to take the splinter out of your brother's eye. Don't give what is holy to dogs or toss your pearls before pigs, or they will trample them under their feet, turn, and tear you to pieces.

"Ask, and it will be given to you. Seek, and you will find. Knock, and the door will be opened to you. For everyone who asks receives, and the one who seeks finds, and to the one who knocks, the door will be opened. Who among you, if his son asks him for bread, will give him a stone? Or if he asks for a fish, will give him a snake? If you then, who are evil, know how to give good gifts to your children, how much more will your Father in heaven give good things to those who ask him."

The Narrow Way

"Therefore, whatever you want others to do for you, do also the same for them, for this is the Law and the Prophets.

"Enter through the narrow gate. For the gate is wide and the road broad that leads to destruction, and there are many who go through it. How narrow is the gate and difficult the road that leads to life, and few find it.

"Be on your guard against false prophets who come to you in sheep's clothing but inwardly are ravaging wolves. You'll recognize them by their fruit. Are grapes gathered from thornbushes or figs from thistles? In the same way, every good tree produces good fruit, but a bad tree produces bad fruit. For each tree is known by its own fruit. Figs aren't gathered from thornbushes, or grapes picked from a bramble bush. A good tree can't produce bad fruit; neither can a bad tree produce good fruit. Every tree that doesn't produce good fruit is cut down and thrown into the fire. A good person produces good out of the good stored up in his heart. An evil person produces evil out of the evil stored up in his heart, for his mouth speaks from the overflow of the heart. So you'll recognize them by their fruit."

A Sure Foundation

"Why do you call me 'Lord, Lord,' and don't do the things I say? Not everyone who says to me, 'Lord, Lord,' will enter the kingdom of heaven, but only the one who does the will of my Father in heaven. On that day many will say to me, 'Lord, Lord, didn't we prophesy in your name, drive out demons in your name, and do many miracles in your name?' Then I will announce to them, 'I never knew you. Depart from me, you lawbreakers!'

"Therefore, everyone who hears these words of mine and acts on them will be like a wise man who built his house on the rock. The rain fell, the rivers rose, and the winds blew and pounded that house. Yet it didn't collapse, because its foundation was on the rock. But everyone who hears these words of mine and doesn't act on them will be like a foolish man who built his house on the sand. The rain fell, the rivers rose, the winds blew and pounded that house, and it collapsed. And the destruction of that house was great. It collapsed with a great crash."

When Jesus had finished saying these things, the crowds were astonished at his teaching, because he was teaching them like one who had authority, and not like their scribes. When he came down from the mountain, large crowds followed him.

A Centurion's Servant Is Healed

A centurion's servant, who was highly valued by him, was sick, paralyzed, in terrible agony, and about to die. When the centurion heard about Jesus, he sent some Jewish elders to him, requesting him to come and save the life of his servant. When they reached Jesus, they pleaded with him earnestly, saying, "He is worthy for you to grant this, because he loves our nation and has built us a synagogue."

Jesus went with them, and when he was not far from the house, the centurion sent friends to tell him, "Lord, don't trouble yourself, since I am not worthy to have you come under my roof. That is why I didn't even consider myself worthy to come to you. But say the word, and my servant will be healed. For I too am a man placed under authority, having soldiers under my command. I say to this one, 'Go,' and he goes; and to another, 'Come,' and he comes; and to my servant, 'Do this,' and he does it."

Hearing this, Jesus was amazed and said to those following him, "Truly I tell you, I have not found anyone in Israel with so great a faith. I tell you that many will come from east and west to share the banquet with Abraham, Isaac, and Jacob in the kingdom of heaven. But the sons of the kingdom will be thrown into the outer darkness where there will be weeping and gnashing of teeth." Then Jesus told the centurion, "Go. As you have believed, let it be done for you." And his servant was healed that very moment.

When those who had been sent returned to the house, they found the servant in good health.

A Widow's Son Is Raised to Life

Afterward he was on his way to a town called Nain. His disciples and a large crowd were traveling with him. Just as he neared the gate of the town, a dead man was being carried out. He was his mother's only son, and she was a widow. A large crowd from the town was also with her. When the Lord saw her, he had compassion on her and said, "Don't weep." Then he came up and touched the open coffin, and the pallbearers stopped. And he said, "Young man, I tell you, get up!"

The dead man sat up and began to speak, and Jesus gave him to his mother. Then fear came over everyone, and they glorified God, saying, "A great prophet has risen among us," and "God has visited his people." This report about him went throughout Judea and all the vicinity.

DAY ELEVEN

Questions from John the Baptist

Then John's disciples told him in prison about all these things Christ was doing. So John summoned two of his disciples and sent them to the Lord, asking, "Are you the one who is to come, or should we expect someone else?"

When the men reached him, they said, "John the Baptist sent us to ask you, 'Are you the one who is to come, or should we expect someone else?'"

At that time Jesus healed many people of diseases, afflictions, and evil spirits, and he granted sight to many blind people. He replied to them, "Go and report to John what you have seen and heard: The blind receive their sight, the lame walk, those with leprosy are cleansed, the deaf hear, the dead are raised, and the poor are told the good news, and blessed is the one who isn't offended by me."

As John's disciples were leaving, he began to speak to the crowds about John: "What did you go out into the wilderness to see? A reed swaying in the wind? What then did you go out to see? A man dressed in soft clothes? See, those who are splendidly dressed and live in luxury are in royal palaces. What then did you go out to see? A prophet? Yes, I tell you, and more than a prophet. This is the one about whom it is written:

> See, I am sending my messenger ahead of you;
> he will prepare your way before you.

I tell you, among those born of women no one is greater than John, but the least in the kingdom of heaven is greater than he."

(And when all the people, including the tax collectors, heard this, they acknowledged God's way of righteousness, because they had been baptized with John's baptism. But since the Pharisees and experts in the law had not been baptized by him, they rejected the plan of God for themselves.)

"From the days of John the Baptist until now," Jesus continued, "the kingdom of heaven has been suffering violence, and the violent have been seizing it by force. For all the prophets and the law prophesied until John. And if you're willing to accept it, he is the Elijah who is to come. Let anyone who has ears listen.

"To what then should I compare the people of this generation, and what are they like? They are like children sitting in the marketplace and calling to each other:

> We played the flute for you,
> but you didn't dance;
> we sang a lament,
> but you didn't weep!

For John the Baptist did not come eating bread or drinking wine, and you say, 'He has a demon!' The Son of Man has come eating and drinking, and you say, 'Look, a glutton and a drunkard, a friend of tax collectors and sinners!' Yet wisdom is vindicated by all her deeds."

Woe to Unrepentant Cities

Then he proceeded to denounce the towns where most of his miracles were done, because they did not repent: "Woe to you, Chorazin! Woe to you, Bethsaida! For if the miracles that were done in you had been done in Tyre and Sidon, they would have repented in sackcloth and ashes long ago. But I tell you, it will be more tolerable for Tyre and Sidon on the day of judgment than for you. And you, Capernaum, will you be exalted to heaven? No, you will go down to Hades. For if the miracles that were done in you had been done in Sodom, it would have remained until today. But I tell you, it will be more tolerable for the land of Sodom on the day of judgment than for you."

At that time Jesus said, "I praise you, Father, Lord of heaven and earth, because you have hidden these things from the wise and intelligent and revealed them to infants. Yes, Father, because this was your good pleasure. All things have been entrusted to me by my Father. No one knows the Son except the Father, and no one knows the Father except the Son and anyone to whom the Son desires to reveal him.

"Come to me, all of you who are weary and burdened, and I will give you rest. Take up my yoke and learn from me, because I am lowly and humble in heart, and you will find rest for your souls. For my yoke is easy and my burden is light."

The Anointing of Jesus' Feet

Then one of the Pharisees invited him to eat with him. He entered the Pharisee's house and reclined at the table. And a woman in the town who was a sinner found out that Jesus was reclining at the table in the Pharisee's house. She brought an alabaster jar of perfume and stood behind him at his feet, weeping, and began to wash his feet with her tears. She wiped his feet with her hair, kissing them and anointing them with the perfume.

When the Pharisee who had invited him saw this, he said to himself, "This man, if he were a prophet, would know who and what kind of woman this is who is touching him—she's a sinner!"

Jesus replied to him, "Simon, I have something to say to you."

He said, "Say it, teacher."

"A creditor had two debtors. One owed five hundred denarii, and the other fifty. Since they could not pay it back, he graciously forgave them both. So, which of them will love him more?"

Simon answered, "I suppose the one he forgave more."

"You have judged correctly," he told him. Turning to the woman, he said to Simon, "Do you see this woman? I entered your house; you gave me no water for my feet, but she, with her tears, has washed my feet and wiped them with her hair. You gave me no kiss, but she hasn't stopped kissing my feet since I came in. You didn't anoint my head with olive oil, but she has anointed my feet with perfume. Therefore I tell you, her many sins have been forgiven; that's why she loved much. But the one who is forgiven little, loves little." Then he said to her, "Your sins are forgiven."

Those who were at the table with him began to say among themselves, "Who is this man who even forgives sins?"

And he said to the woman, "Your faith has saved you. Go in peace."

Afterward he was traveling from one town and village to another, preaching and telling the good news of the kingdom of God. The Twelve were with him, and also some women who had been healed of evil spirits and sicknesses: Mary, called Magdalene (seven demons had come out of her); Joanna the wife of Chuza, Herod's steward; Susanna; and many others who were supporting them from their possessions.

The Spiritual Family of Jesus

While he was still speaking with the crowds, his mother and brothers were standing outside wanting to speak to him, but they could not meet with him because of the crowd. Someone told him, "Look, your mother and your brothers are standing outside, wanting to speak to you."

He replied to the one who was speaking to him, "Who is my mother and who are my brothers?" Looking at those sitting in a circle around him, he stretched out his hand toward his disciples and said, "Here are my mother and my brothers! For whoever hears and does the will of my Father in heaven is my brother and sister and mother."

DAY TWELVE

A Parable of Four Soils

On that day Jesus went out of the house and was sitting by the sea. Such large crowds gathered around him that he got into a boat and sat down, while the whole crowd from every town stood on the shore.

Then he told them many things in parables, saying: "Consider the sower who went out to sow. As he sowed, some seed fell along the path where it was trampled on, and the birds came and devoured them. Other seed fell on rocky ground where it didn't have much soil, and it grew up quickly since the soil wasn't deep. But when the sun came up, it was scorched, and since it had no root, it withered away for lack of moisture. Other seed fell among thorns, and the thorns came up with it and choked it and it didn't produce fruit. Still other seed fell on good ground and produced fruit that increased: some a hundred, some sixty, and some thirty times what was sown." As he said this, he called out, "Let anyone who has ears listen."

When he was alone, those around him with the Twelve asked him, "Why are you speaking to them in parables?"

He answered, "Because the secrets of the kingdom of heaven have been given for you to know, but it has not been given to them. To those outside, everything comes in parables. For whoever has, more will be given to him, and he will have more than enough; but whoever does not have, even what he has will be taken away from him. That is why I speak to them in parables, because

> Looking they may not see,
> and hearing they may not understand.

Isaiah's prophecy is fulfilled in them, which says:

> You will listen and listen,
> but never understand;
> you will look and look,
> but never perceive.
> For this people's heart has grown callous;
> their ears are hard of hearing,
> and they have shut their eyes;
> otherwise they might see with their eyes,
> and hear with their ears, and
> understand with their hearts,
> and turn back—
> and I would heal them.

"Blessed are your eyes because they do see, and your ears because they do hear. For truly I tell you, many prophets and righteous people longed to see the things you see but didn't see them, to hear the things you hear but didn't hear them."

Then he said to them, "Don't you understand this parable? How then will you understand all of the parables? So listen to the parable of the sower: The sower sows the word. When anyone hears the word about the kingdom and doesn't understand it, the evil one (Satan, the devil) comes and snatches away what was sown in his heart so that they may not believe and be saved. This is the one sown along the path. And the one sown on rocky ground—this is one who hears the word and immediately receives it with joy. But he has no root and is short-lived. When distress or persecution, a time of testing, comes because of the word, immediately he falls away. Now the one sown among the thorns—this is one who hears the word, but the worries of this age and the deceitfulness of wealth and pleasures of life enter in and choke the word, and it becomes unfruitful and produces no mature fruit. But the one sown on the good ground—this is one who hears with an honest and good heart and understands the word and welcomes it, who does produce fruit and yields: some a hundred, some sixty, some thirty times what was sown."

He also said to them, "No one, after lighting a lamp, covers it with a basket or puts it under a bed, but puts it on a lampstand so that those who come in may see its light. For nothing is concealed that won't be revealed, and nothing hidden that won't be made known and brought to light. If anyone has ears to hear, let him listen. Therefore take care how you listen. By the measure you use, it will be measured to you—and more will be added to you. For whoever has, more will be given to him; and whoever does not have, even what he thinks he has will be taken away from him."

Parables of Weeds, Seeds, and Leaven

"The kingdom of God is like this," he said. "A man scatters seed on the ground. He sleeps and rises night and day; the seed sprouts and grows, although he doesn't know how. The soil produces a crop by itself—first the blade, then the head, and then the full grain on the head. As soon as the crop is ready, he sends for the sickle, because the harvest has come."

He presented another parable to them: "The kingdom of heaven may be compared to a man who sowed good seed in his field. But while people were sleeping, his enemy came, sowed weeds among the wheat, and left. When the plants sprouted and produced grain, then the weeds also appeared. The landowner's servants came to him and said, 'Master, didn't you sow good seed in your field? Then where did the weeds come from?'

"'An enemy did this,' he told them.

"'So, do you want us to go and pull them up?' the servants asked him.

"'No,' he said. 'When you pull up the weeds, you might also uproot the wheat with them. Let both grow together until the harvest. At harvest time I'll tell the reapers: Gather the weeds first and tie them in bundles to burn them, but collect the wheat in my barn.'"

And he said, "With what can we compare the kingdom of heaven, or what parable can we use to describe it? It's like a mustard seed that, when sown upon the soil, is the smallest of all the seeds on the ground. And when sown, it comes up and grows taller than all the garden plants, and produces large branches, so that the birds of the sky can nest in its shade or branches."

He told them another parable: "The kingdom of heaven is like leaven that a woman took and mixed into fifty pounds of flour until all of it was leavened."

He was speaking the word to them with many parables like these, as they were able to understand. He did not speak to them without a parable, so that what was spoken through the prophet might be fulfilled:

"I will open my mouth in parables;
I will declare things kept secret
from the foundation of the world."

Privately, however, he explained everything to his own disciples.

Then he left the crowds and went into the house. His disciples approached him and said, "Explain to us the parable of the weeds in the field."

He replied, "The one who sows the good seed is the Son of Man; the field is the world; and the good seed—these are the children of the kingdom. The weeds are the children of the evil one, and the enemy who sowed them is the devil. The harvest is the end of

the age, and the harvesters are angels. Therefore, just as
the weeds are gathered and burned in the fire, so it will
be at the end of the age. The Son of Man will send out
his angels, and they will gather from his kingdom all
who cause sin and those guilty of lawlessness. They will
throw them into the blazing furnace where there will
be weeping and gnashing of teeth. Then the righteous
will shine like the sun in their Father's kingdom. Let
anyone who has ears listen."

Parables of Treasure, a Pearl, and Fish Nets

"The kingdom of heaven is like treasure, buried in a
field, that a man found and reburied. Then in his joy
he goes and sells everything he has and buys that field.

"Again, the kingdom of heaven is like a merchant
in search of fine pearls. When he found one priceless
pearl, he went and sold everything he had and bought it.

"Again, the kingdom of heaven is like a large net
thrown into the sea. It collected every kind of fish, and
when it was full, they dragged it ashore, sat down, and
gathered the good fish into containers, but threw out
the worthless ones. So it will be at the end of the age.
The angels will go out, separate the evil people from the
righteous, and throw them into the blazing furnace,
where there will be weeping and gnashing of teeth.

"Have you understood all these things?"

They answered him, "Yes."

"Therefore," he said to them, "every teacher of
the law who has become a disciple in the kingdom of

heaven is like the owner of a house who brings out of his storeroom treasures new and old."

When Jesus had finished these parables, he left there.

DAY
THIRTEEN

Calming the Storm

When Jesus saw a large crowd around him, he gave the order to go to the other side of the sea. As he got into the boat, his disciples followed him. Suddenly, a violent storm arose on the sea, so that the boat was being swamped by the waves—but Jesus kept sleeping. So the disciples came and woke him up, saying, "Lord, save us! Teacher! Master, Master, don't you care that we're going to die?"

He got up, rebuked the wind, and said to the sea, "Silence! Be still!" The wind ceased, and there was a great calm. Then he said to them, "Why are you afraid? Do you still have no faith?"

And they were amazed and terrified and asked one another, "Who then is this? What kind of man is this? Even the wind and the sea obey him!"

Casting Out Demons

They came to the other side of the sea, to the region of the Gerasenes, which is opposite Galilee. As soon as Jesus got out of the boat, two demon-possessed men from the town came out of the tombs and met him. One of them, for a long time, had worn no clothes and did not stay in a house but in the tombs, and no one was able to restrain him anymore—not even with a chain—because he often had been bound with shackles and chains, but had torn the chains apart and smashed the shackles. No one was strong enough to subdue him. So violent that no one could pass that way. Night and day among the tombs and on the mountains, he was always crying out and cutting himself with stones.

When he saw Jesus from a distance, he ran and knelt down before him. And he cried out with a loud voice, "What do you have to do with me, Jesus, Son of the Most High God? I beg you before God, don't torment me!" For he had told him, "Come out of the man, you unclean spirit!"

"What is your name?" he asked him.

"My name is Legion," he answered him, "because we are many." And he begged him earnestly not to send them out of the region.

A long way off from them, a large herd of pigs was there, feeding on the hillside. The demons begged him, "If you drive us out, send us to the pigs, so that we may enter them." So he gave them permission, and the unclean spirits came out and entered the pigs. The herd of about two thousand rushed down the steep bank into the sea and drowned there.

The men who tended them ran off and reported it in the town and the countryside. At that, the whole town went out to meet Jesus. They came to Jesus and saw the man who had been demon-possessed, sitting at Jesus' feet, dressed and in his right mind; and they were afraid. Those who had seen it described to them what had happened to the demon-possessed man and told about the pigs. Then they began to beg him to leave their region because they were gripped by great fear.

As he was getting into the boat, the man who had been demon-possessed begged him earnestly that he might remain with him. Jesus did not let him but told him, "Go home to your own people, and report to them how much the Lord has done for you and how he has had mercy on you." So he went out and began to proclaim in the Decapolis how much Jesus had done for him, and they were all amazed.

Healing the Sick, the Blind, and the Possessed

When Jesus had crossed over again by boat to the other side, a large crowd gathered around him while he was by the sea for they were all expecting him. One of the synagogue leaders, named Jairus, came, and when he saw Jesus, he fell at his feet and begged him earnestly to come to his house, "My little daughter, about twelve years old, is dying. Come and lay your hands on her so that she can get well and live." So Jesus went with him, and a large crowd was following and pressing against him nearly crushing him.

Now a woman suffering from bleeding for twelve years had endured much under many doctors. She had spent everything she had and was not helped at all. On the contrary, she became worse. Having heard about Jesus, she came up behind him in the crowd and touched end of his robe. For she said, "If I just touch his clothes, I'll be made well." Instantly her flow of blood ceased, and she sensed in her body that she was healed of her affliction.

Immediately Jesus realized that power had gone out from him. He turned around in the crowd and said, "Who touched my clothes?"

His disciples said to him, "You see the crowd pressing against you, and yet you say, 'Who touched me?'"

"Someone did touch me," said Jesus. "I know that power has gone out from me."

But he was looking around to see who had done this. The woman, with fear and trembling, knowing what had happened to her, came and fell down before him, and told him the whole truth. "Daughter," he said to her, "your faith has saved you. Go in peace and be healed from your affliction."

While he was still speaking, people came from the synagogue leader's house and said to Jairus, "Your daughter is dead. Why bother the teacher anymore?"

When Jesus overheard what was said, he told the synagogue leader, "Don't be afraid. Only believe and she will be saved." He did not let anyone accompany him except Peter, James, and John, James's brother and the child's father and mother. They came to the leader's house, and he saw a commotion—people weeping and wailing loudly and the flute players. He went in and said to them, "Why are you making a commotion and weeping? Stop crying. Leave, because the child is not dead but asleep." They laughed at him, because they knew she was dead, but he put them all outside.

He took the child's father, mother, and those who were with him, and entered the place where the child was. Then he took the child by the hand and said to her, "*Talitha koum*" (which is translated, "Little girl, I say to you, get up"). Immediately her spirit returned, and she got up at once and began to walk. At this they were utterly astounded. Then he gave them strict orders that no one should know about this and told them to give her something to eat.

Then news of this spread throughout that whole area.

As Jesus went on from there, two blind men followed him, calling out, "Have mercy on us, Son of David!"

When he entered the house, the blind men approached him, and Jesus said to them, "Do you believe that I can do this?"

They said to him, "Yes, Lord."

Then he touched their eyes, saying, "Let it be done for you according to your faith." And their eyes were opened. Then Jesus warned them sternly, "Be sure that no one finds out." But they went out and spread the news about him throughout that whole area.

Just as they were going out, a demon-possessed man who was unable to speak was brought to him. When the demon had been driven out, the man who had been mute spoke, and the crowds were amazed, saying, "Nothing like this has ever been seen in Israel!"

But the Pharisees said, "He drives out demons by the ruler of the demons."

A Final Visit to His Hometown

Jesus left there and came to his hometown, and his disciples followed him. When the Sabbath came, he began to teach in the synagogue, and many who heard him were astonished. "Where did this man get these things?" they said. "What is this wisdom that has been given to him, and how are these miracles performed by his hands? Isn't this the carpenter, the son of Mary, and the brother of James, Joses, Judas, and Simon? And aren't his sisters here with us?" So they were offended by him.

Jesus said to them, "A prophet is not without honor except in his hometown, among his relatives, and in his household." He was not able to do a miracle there, except that he laid his hands on a few sick people and healed them. And he was amazed at their unbelief.

DAY
FOURTEEN

Workers for the Harvest

Jesus continued going around to all the towns and villages, teaching in their synagogues, preaching the good news of the kingdom, and healing every disease and every sickness. When he saw the crowds, he felt compassion for them, because they were distressed and dejected, like sheep without a shepherd. Then he said to his disciples, "The harvest is abundant, but the workers are few. Therefore, pray to the Lord of the harvest to send out workers into his harvest."

Summoning his twelve disciples, he sent them out in pairs to proclaim the kingdom of God. He gave them power and authority over unclean spirits, to drive them out and to heal every disease and sickness.

These are the names of the twelve apostles: First, Simon, who is called Peter, and Andrew his brother; James the son of Zebedee, and John his brother; Philip and Bartholomew; Thomas and Matthew the tax collector; James the son of Alphaeus, and Thaddaeus; Simon the Zealot, and Judas Iscariot, who also betrayed him.

Jesus sent out these twelve after giving them instructions: "Don't take the road that leads to the

Gentiles, and don't enter any Samaritan town. Instead, go to the lost sheep of the house of Israel. As you go, proclaim, 'The kingdom of heaven has come near.' Heal the sick, raise the dead, cleanse those with leprosy, drive out demons. Freely you received, freely give. Don't acquire gold, silver, or copper for your money-belts. Take nothing for the road except a staff—no traveling bag, no bread, no money in your belts. Wear sandals but don't take an extra shirt, for the worker is worthy of his food. When you enter any town or village, find out who is worthy, and stay there until you leave. Greet a household when you enter it, and if the household is worthy, let your peace be on it; but if it is unworthy, let your peace return to you. If anyone does not welcome you or listen to your words, shake the dust off your feet when you leave that house or town as a testimony against them. Truly I tell you, it will be more tolerable on the day of judgment for the land of Sodom and Gomorrah than for that town.

"Look, I'm sending you out like sheep among wolves. Therefore be as shrewd as serpents and as innocent as doves. Beware of them, because they will hand you over to local courts and flog you in their synagogues. You will even be brought before governors and kings because of me, to bear witness to them and to the Gentiles. But when they hand you over, don't worry about how or what you are to speak. For you will be given what to say at that hour, because it isn't you speaking, but the Spirit of your Father is speaking through you.

"Brother will betray brother to death, and a father his child. Children will rise up against parents and have them put to death. You will be hated by everyone because of my name. But the one who endures to the end will be saved. When they persecute you in one town, flee to another. For truly I tell you, you will not have gone through the towns of Israel before the Son of Man comes. A disciple is not above his teacher, or a slave above his master. It is enough for a disciple to become like his teacher and a slave like his master. If they called the head of the house 'Beelzebul,' how much more the members of his household!

"Therefore, don't be afraid of them, since there is nothing covered that won't be uncovered and nothing hidden that won't be made known. What I tell you in the dark, speak in the light. What you hear in a whisper, proclaim on the housetops. Don't fear those who kill the body but are not able to kill the soul; rather, fear him who is able to destroy both soul and body in hell. Aren't two sparrows sold for a penny? Yet not one of them falls to the ground without your Father's consent. But even the hairs of your head have all been counted. So don't be afraid; you are worth more than many sparrows.

"Therefore, everyone who will acknowledge me before others, I will also acknowledge him before my Father in heaven. But whoever denies me before others, I will also deny him before my Father in heaven. Don't assume that I came to bring peace on the earth. I did not come to bring peace, but a sword. For I came to turn

> a man against his father,
> a daughter against her mother,
> a daughter-in-law against her mother-in-law;
> and a man's enemies will be
> the members of his household.

The one who loves a father or mother more than me is not worthy of me; the one who loves a son or daughter more than me is not worthy of me. And whoever doesn't take up his cross and follow me is not worthy of me. Anyone who finds his life will lose it, and anyone who loses his life because of me will find it.

"The one who welcomes you welcomes me, and the one who welcomes me welcomes him who sent me. Anyone who welcomes a prophet because he is a prophet will receive a prophet's reward. And anyone who welcomes a righteous person because he's righteous will receive a righteous person's reward. And whoever gives even a cup of cold water to one of these little ones because he is a disciple, truly I tell you, he will never lose his reward."

So they went out and preached that people should repent. They drove out many demons, anointed many sick people with oil and healed them.

The Death of John the Baptist

At that time King Herod (Antipas, the tetrarch) heard about it, because Jesus's name had become well known. He was perplexed, because some said, "John the Baptist has been raised from the dead, and that's why miraculous powers are at work in him." But others said, "He's Elijah." Still others said, "He's a prophet, like one of the prophets from long ago."

When Herod heard of it, he said, "John, the one I beheaded, has been raised!" And he wanted to see him.

For Herod himself had given orders to arrest John and to chain him in prison on account of Herodias, his brother Philip's wife, because he had married her. John had been telling Herod, "It is not lawful for you to have your brother's wife." So Herodias held a grudge against him and wanted to kill him. But she could not, because Herod feared John and protected him, knowing he was a righteous and holy man. When Herod heard him he would be very perplexed, and yet he liked to listen to him. Though Herod wanted to kill John, he feared the crowd since they regarded John as a prophet.

An opportune time came on his birthday, when Herod gave a banquet for his nobles, military commanders, and the leading men of Galilee. When Herodias's own daughter came in and danced, she pleased Herod and his guests. The king said to the girl, "Ask me whatever you want, and I'll give it to you." He promised her with an oath: "Whatever you ask me I will give you, up to half my kingdom."

She went out and said to her mother, "What should I ask for?"

"John the Baptist's head," she said.

At once she hurried to the king and said, "I want you to give me John the Baptist's head on a platter immediately." Although the king was deeply distressed, because of his oaths and the guests he did not want to refuse her. The king immediately sent for an executioner and commanded him to bring John's head. So he went and beheaded him in prison, brought his head on a platter, and gave it to the girl. Then the girl gave it to her mother. When John's disciples heard about it, they came and removed his corpse and placed it in a tomb, and went and reported to Jesus.

An Attempt to Rest

The apostles gathered around Jesus and reported to him all that they had done and taught. He said to them, "Come away by yourselves to a remote place and rest for a while." For many people were coming and going, and they did not even have time to eat.

So they went away in the boat by themselves to a remote place across the Sea of Galilee (or Tiberias) to a town called Bethsaida. But many saw them leaving and recognized them, and they ran on foot from all the towns and arrived ahead of them because they saw the signs that he was performing by healing the sick. When he went ashore, he saw a large crowd. He welcomed them and had compassion on them, because they were like sheep without a shepherd. So Jesus went up a mountain and sat down there with his disciples and began to teach them many things about the kingdom of God, and healed those who needed healing.

Feeding the Five Thousand

Now the Passover, a Jewish festival, was near. So when Jesus looked up and noticed a huge crowd coming toward him, he asked Philip, "Where will we buy bread so that these people can eat?" He asked this to test him, for he himself knew what he was going to do.

Philip answered him, "Two hundred denarii worth of bread wouldn't be enough for each of them to have a little."

One of his disciples, Andrew, Simon Peter's brother, said to him, "There's a boy here who has five barley loaves and two fish—but what are they for so many?"

His disciples approached him and said, "This place is deserted, and it is already late. Send them away so that they can go into the surrounding countryside and villages to buy themselves something to eat."

"They don't need to go away," Jesus told them. "You give them something to eat."

They said to him, "Should we go and buy two hundred denarii worth of bread and give them something to eat?"

He asked them, "How many loaves do you have? Go and see."

"We have no more than five loaves and two fish," they said, "unless we go and buy food for all these people."

"Bring them here to me," he said.

Jesus said, "Have the people sit down." Then he instructed them to have all the people sit down in groups on the green grass. So they sat down in groups of hundreds and fifties.

He took the five loaves and the two fish, and looking up to heaven, he blessed them. After giving thanks he broke the loaves and kept giving them to his disciples to set before the people. He also divided the two fish among them all, as much as they wanted. Everyone ate and was satisfied.

When they were full, he told his disciples, "Collect the leftovers so that nothing is wasted." So they collected them and filled twelve baskets with the pieces from the five barley loaves that were left over by those who had eaten. Now those who ate were about five thousand men, besides women and children.

When the people saw the sign he had done, they said, "This truly is the Prophet who is to come into the world."

Therefore, Jesus realized that they were about to come and take him by force to make him king. Immediately he made his disciples get into the boat and go ahead of him to the other side, while he dismissed the crowd. After he said good-bye to them, he went away to the mountain to pray. Well into the night, he was there alone.

Walking on the Water

His disciples went down to the sea, got into a boat, and started across the sea to Capernaum. Darkness had already set in, but Jesus had not yet come to them. A high wind arose, and the sea began to churn.

Jesus was alone on the land, the boat was in the middle of the sea some distance from land, and he saw them straining at the oars, battered by the waves because the wind was against them. Very early in the morning, after they had rowed about three or four miles, they saw Jesus walking on the sea. He came toward them walking on the sea and wanted to pass by them.

When the disciples saw him walking on the sea, they were terrified. "It's a ghost!" they said, and they cried out in fear.

Immediately Jesus spoke to them. "Have courage! It is I. Don't be afraid."

"Lord, if it's you," Peter answered him, "command me to come to you on the water."

He said, "Come."

And climbing out of the boat, Peter started walking on the water and came toward Jesus. But when he saw the strength of the wind, he was afraid, and beginning to sink he cried out, "Lord, save me!"

Immediately Jesus reached out his hand, caught hold of him, and said to him, "You of little faith, why did you doubt?"

When they got into the boat, the wind ceased. They were completely astounded, because they had not understood about the loaves. Instead, their hearts were hardened. Then those in the boat worshiped him and said, "Truly you are the Son of God."

When they had crossed over, they came to shore at Gennesaret. When the men of that place recognized him, they alerted the whole vicinity and brought to him all who were sick. They begged him that they might only touch the end of his robe, and as many as touched it were healed. They hurried throughout that region and began to carry the sick on mats to wherever they heard he was. Wherever he went, into villages, towns, or the country, they laid the sick in the marketplaces and begged him that they might touch just the end of his robe. And everyone who touched it was healed.

The Bread of Life

The next day, the crowd that had stayed on the other side of the sea saw there had been only one boat. They also saw that Jesus had not boarded the boat with his disciples, but that his disciples had gone off alone. Some boats from Tiberias came near the place where they had eaten the bread after the Lord had given thanks. When the crowd saw that neither Jesus nor his disciples were there, they got into the boats and went to Capernaum looking for Jesus. When they found him on the other side of the sea, they said to him, "Rabbi, when did you get here?"

Jesus answered, "Truly I tell you, you are looking for me, not because you saw the signs, but because you ate the loaves and were filled. Don't work for the food that perishes but for the food that lasts for eternal life, which the Son of Man will give you, because God the Father has set his seal of approval on him."

"What can we do to perform the works of God?" they asked.

Jesus replied, "This is the work of God—that you believe in the one he has sent."

"What sign, then, are you going to do so that we may see and believe you?" they asked. "What are you going to perform? Our ancestors ate the manna in the wilderness, just as it is written: *He gave them bread from heaven to eat.*"

Jesus said to them, "Truly I tell you, Moses didn't give you the bread from heaven, but my Father gives you the true bread from heaven. For the bread of God is the one who comes down from heaven and gives life to the world."

Then they said, "Sir, give us this bread always."

"I am the bread of life," Jesus told them. "No one who comes to me will ever be hungry, and no one who believes in me will ever be thirsty again. But as I told you, you've seen me, and yet you do not believe. Everyone the Father gives me will come to me, and the one who comes to me I will never cast out. For I have come down from heaven, not to do my own will, but the will of him who sent me. This is the will of him who sent me: that I should lose none of those he has given me but should raise them up on the last day. For this is the will of my Father: that everyone who sees the Son and believes in him will have eternal life, and I will raise him up on the last day."

Therefore the Jews started grumbling about him because he said, "I am the bread that came down from heaven." They were saying, "Isn't this Jesus the son of Joseph, whose father and mother we know? How can he now say, 'I have come down from heaven'?"

Jesus answered them, "Stop grumbling among yourselves. No one can come to me unless the Father who sent me draws him, and I will raise him up on the last day. It is written in the Prophets: *And they will all be taught by God*. Everyone who has listened to and learned from the Father comes to me—not that anyone has seen the Father except the one who is from God. He has seen the Father.

"Truly I tell you, anyone who believes has eternal life. I am the bread of life. Your ancestors ate the manna in the wilderness, and they died. This is the bread that comes down from heaven so that anyone may eat of it and not die. I am the living bread that came down from heaven. If anyone eats of this bread he will live forever. The bread that I will give for the life of the world is my flesh."

At that, the Jews argued among themselves, "How can this man give us his flesh to eat?"

So Jesus said to them, "Truly I tell you, unless you eat the flesh of the Son of Man and drink his blood, you do not have life in yourselves. The one who eats my flesh and drinks my blood has eternal life, and I will raise him up on the last day, because my flesh is true food and my blood is true drink. The one who eats my flesh and drinks my blood remains in me, and I in him. Just as the living Father sent me and I live because of the Father, so the one who feeds on me will live because of me. This is the bread that came down from heaven; it is not like the manna your ancestors ate—and they died. The one who eats this bread will live forever."

He said these things while teaching in the synagogue in Capernaum.

DAY
SIXTEEN

Some Walk Away

Therefore, when many of his disciples heard this, they said, "This teaching is hard. Who can accept it?"

Jesus, knowing in himself that his disciples were grumbling about this, asked them, "Does this offend you? Then what if you were to observe the Son of Man ascending to where he was before? The Spirit is the one who gives life. The flesh doesn't help at all. The words that I have spoken to you are spirit and are life. But there are some among you who don't believe." (For Jesus knew from the beginning those who did not believe and the one who would betray him.) He said, "This is why I told you that no one can come to me unless it is granted to him by the Father."

From that moment many of his disciples turned back and no longer accompanied him. So Jesus said to the Twelve, "You don't want to go away too, do you?"

Simon Peter answered, "Lord, to whom will we go? You have the words of eternal life. We have come to believe and know that you are the Holy One of God."

Jesus replied to them, "Didn't I choose you, the Twelve? Yet one of you is a devil." He was referring to

Judas, Simon Iscariot's son, one of the Twelve, because he was going to betray him.

The Brothers of Jesus Do Not Believe

After this, Jesus traveled in Galilee, since he did not want to travel in Judea because the Jews were trying to kill him. The Jewish Festival of Shelters (or Tabernacles) was near. So his brothers said to him, "Leave here and go to Judea so that your disciples can see your works that you are doing. For no one does anything in secret while he's seeking public recognition. If you do these things, show yourself to the world." (For not even his brothers believed in him.)

Jesus told them, "My time has not yet arrived, but your time is always at hand. The world cannot hate you, but it does hate me because I testify about it— that its works are evil. Go up to the festival yourselves. I'm not going up to this festival, because my time has not yet fully come." After he had said these things, he stayed in Galilee.

Jesus Breaks Religious Traditions

The Pharisees and some of the scribes who had come from Jerusalem gathered around him. They observed that some of his disciples were eating bread with unclean—that is, unwashed—hands. (For the Pharisees and all the Jews do not eat unless they give their hands a ceremonial washing, keeping the tradition of the elders. When they come from the marketplace, they do not eat unless they have washed. And there are many other customs they have received and keep, like the washing of cups, pitchers, kettles, and dining couches.) So the Pharisees and the scribes asked him, "Why don't your disciples live according to the tradition of the elders, instead of eating bread with ceremonially unclean hands? They don't wash their hands when they eat."

He answered them, "Isaiah prophesied correctly about you hypocrites, as it is written:

This people honors me with their lips,
but their heart is far from me.
They worship me in vain,
teaching as doctrines human commands.

Abandoning the command of God, you hold on to human tradition." He also said to them, "You have a fine way of invalidating God's command in order to set up your tradition! For Moses proclaimed God's commands: Honor your father and your mother; and Whoever speaks evil of father or mother must be put to death. But you say, 'If anyone tells his father or mother: Whatever benefit you might have received from me is *corban*'" (that is, an offering devoted to God), "you no longer let him do anything for his father or mother. You nullify the word of God by your tradition that you have handed down. And you do many other similar things."

Summoning the crowd again, he told them, "Listen and understand: It's not what goes into the mouth that defiles a person, but what comes out of the mouth—this defiles a person."

Then the disciples came up and told him, "Do you know that the Pharisees took offense when they heard what you said?"

He replied, "Every plant that my heavenly Father didn't plant will be uprooted. Leave them alone! They are blind guides. And if the blind guide the blind, both will fall into a pit."

When he went into the house away from the crowd, Peter and the disciples said, "Explain this parable to us."

"Do you still lack understanding?" he asked. "Don't you realize that whatever goes into the mouth passes into the stomach and is eliminated?" (Thus he declared all foods clean.) "But what comes out of the mouth comes from the heart, and this defiles a person. For from within, out of people's hearts, come evil thoughts, sexual immoralities, thefts, murders, adulteries, greed, evil actions, deceit, self-indulgence, envy, slander, pride, and foolishness. All these evil things come from within and defile a person."

Jesus and a Gentile Woman

When Jesus left there, he withdrew to the area of Tyre and Sidon. He entered a house and did not want anyone to know it, but he could not escape notice.

Instead, immediately after hearing about him, a Canaanite woman, a Gentile, Syrophoenician by birth, from that region, came and kept crying out, "Have mercy on me, Lord, Son of David! My daughter is severely tormented by a demon."

Jesus did not say a word to her. His disciples approached him and urged him, "Send her away because she's crying out after us."

He replied, "I was sent only to the lost sheep of the house of Israel."

But she came, knelt before him and fell at his feet, and said, "Lord, help me!" She was asking him to cast the demon out of her daughter.

He answered, "Let the children be fed first, because it isn't right to take the children's bread and throw it to the dogs."

"Yes, Lord," she said, "yet even the dogs eat the children's crumbs that fall from their masters' table."

Then he told her, "Woman, your faith is great. Let it be done for you as you want. Because of this reply, you may go. The demon has left your daughter." And from that moment her daughter was healed. When she went back to her home, she found her child lying on the bed, and the demon was gone.

Healings in the Decapolis

Again, leaving the region of Tyre, he went by way of Sidon to the Sea of Galilee, through the region of the Decapolis.

He went up on a mountain and sat there. They brought to him a deaf man who had difficulty speaking and begged Jesus to lay his hand on him. So he took him away from the crowd in private. After putting his fingers in the man's ears and spitting, he touched his tongue. Looking up to heaven, he sighed deeply and said to him, "*Ephphatha!*" (that is, "Be opened!"). Immediately his ears were opened, his tongue was loosened, and he began to speak clearly. He ordered them to tell no one, but the more he ordered them, the more they proclaimed it.

They were extremely astonished and said, "He has done everything well. He even makes the deaf hear and the mute speak."

Large crowds came to him, including the lame, the blind, the crippled, those unable to speak, and many others. They put them at his feet, and he healed them. So the crowd was amazed when they saw those unable to speak talking, the crippled restored, the lame walking, and the blind seeing, and they gave glory to the God of Israel.

Feeding the Four Thousand in the Decapolis

In those days there was again a large crowd, and they had nothing to eat. He called the disciples and said to them, "I have compassion on the crowd, because they've already stayed with me three days and have nothing to eat. If I send them home hungry, they will collapse on the way, and some of them have come a long distance."

His disciples answered him, "Where can anyone get enough bread here in this desolate place to feed these people?"

How many loaves do you have?" he asked them.

"Seven," they said, "and a few small fish." He commanded the crowd to sit down on the ground. Taking the seven loaves, he gave thanks, broke them, and gave them to his disciples to set before the people. So they served them to the crowd. They also had a few small fish, and after he had blessed them, he said these were to be served as well. They ate and were satisfied. Then they collected seven large baskets of leftover pieces. About four thousand were there besides women and children.

DAY SEVENTEEN

Demanding a Miracle

After dismissing the crowds, he got into the boat with his disciples and went to the region of Magadan, the district of Dalmanutha.

The Pharisees and Sadducees approached and began to argue with him, demanding of him a sign from heaven to test him. He sighed deeply in his spirit and replied, "When evening comes you say, 'It will be good weather because the sky is red.' And in the morning, 'Today will be stormy because the sky is red and threatening.' You know how to read the appearance of the sky, but you can't read the signs of the times. Why does this evil and adulterous generation demand a sign? Truly I tell you, no sign will be given to this generation except the sign of Jonah."

Then he left them, got back into the boat, and went to the other side. The disciples had forgotten to take bread and had only one loaf with them in the boat. Then he gave them strict orders: "Watch out! Beware of the leaven of the Pharisees and Sadducees and the leaven of Herod." They were discussing among themselves, "We didn't bring any bread."

Aware of this, he said to them, "Why are you discussing the fact you have no bread? You of little faith. Don't you understand or comprehend yet? Do you have hardened hearts? Do you have eyes and not see; do you have ears and not hear? And do you not remember? When I broke the five loaves for the five thousand, how many baskets full of leftovers did you collect?"

"Twelve," they told him.

"When I broke the seven loaves for the four thousand, how many baskets full of pieces did you collect?

"Seven," they said.

And he said to them, "Don't you understand yet?

"Why is it you don't understand that when I told you, 'Beware of the leaven of the Pharisees and Sadducees,' it wasn't about bread?" Then they understood that he had not told them to beware of the leaven in bread, but of the teaching of the Pharisees and Sadducees.

They came to Bethsaida. They brought a blind man to him and begged him to touch him. He took the blind man by the hand and brought him out of the village. Spitting on his eyes and laying his hands on him, he asked him, "Do you see anything?"

He looked up and said, "I see people—they look like trees walking."

Again Jesus placed his hands on the man's eyes. The man looked intently and his sight was restored and he saw everything clearly. Then he sent him home, saying, "Don't even go into the village."

Peter's Great Confession

Jesus came to the region and villages of Caesarea Philippi. On the road he was praying in private, and his disciples were with him. He asked his disciples, "Who do people say that the Son of Man is?"

They replied, "Some say John the Baptist; others, Elijah; still others, Jeremiah or one of the ancient prophets who has come back."

"But you," he asked them, "who do you say that I am?"

Simon Peter answered, "You are the Messiah, the Son of the living God."

Jesus responded, "Blessed are you, Simon son of Jonah, because flesh and blood did not reveal this to you, but my Father in heaven. And I also say to you that you are Peter, and on this rock I will build my church, and the gates of Hades will not overpower it. I will give you the keys of the kingdom of heaven, and whatever you bind on earth will have been bound in heaven, and whatever you loose on earth will have been loosed in heaven." Then he strictly warned and instructed the disciples to tell no one that he was the Messiah.

Jesus Prophesies His Death and Resurrection

From then on Jesus began to point out to his disciples that it was necessary for him to go to Jerusalem and be rejected and suffer many things from the elders, chief priests, and scribes, be killed, and be raised the third day. He spoke openly about this. Peter took him aside and began to rebuke him, "Oh no, Lord! This will never happen to you!"

Jesus turned and rebuked Peter, "Get behind me, Satan! You are a hindrance to me because you're not thinking about God's concerns but human concerns."

Take Up Your Cross

Calling the crowd along with his disciples, he said to them, "If anyone wants to follow after me, let him deny himself, take up his cross daily, and follow me. For whoever wants to save his life will lose it, but whoever loses his life because of me and the gospel will save it. For what does it benefit someone to gain the whole world and yet lose his life? What can anyone give in exchange for his life? For whoever is ashamed of me and my words in this adulterous and sinful generation, the Son of Man will also be ashamed of him when he comes in his glory and the glory of his Father with the holy angels, and then he will reward each according to what he has done."

Then he said to them, "Truly I tell you, there are some standing here who will not taste death until they see the Son of Man coming in his kingdom with power."

The Transfiguration of Jesus

About six days after this conversation, he took along Peter, John, and James and went up on the high mountain to pray and be alone.

As he was praying, he was transfigured in front of them. The appearance of his face changed and shone like the sun, his clothes became dazzling as white as the light—extremely white as no launderer on earth could whiten them. Suddenly, two men were talking with him—Moses and Elijah. They appeared in glory and were speaking of his departure, which he was about to accomplish in Jerusalem.

Peter and those with him were in a deep sleep, and when they became fully awake, they saw his glory and the two men who were standing with him.

As the two men were departing from him, Peter said to Jesus, "Lord, it's good for us to be here. If you want, I will set up three shelters here: one for you, one for Moses, and one for Elijah"—because he did not know what to say, since they were terrified.

While he was still speaking, suddenly a bright cloud covered them, and a voice from the cloud said, "This is my beloved Son, with whom I am well-pleased. Listen to him!" When the disciples heard this, they fell facedown and were terrified.

Jesus came up, touched them, and said, "Get up; don't be afraid." When they looked up they saw no one except Jesus alone.

As they were coming down the mountain, Jesus commanded them, "Don't tell anyone about the vision until the Son of Man is raised from the dead." They kept this word to themselves, and at that time told no one what they had seen, questioning what "rising from the dead" meant.

So the disciples asked him, "Why then do the scribes say that Elijah must come first?"

"Elijah is coming and will restore everything," he replied. "But I tell you: Elijah has already come, and they didn't recognize him. On the contrary, they did whatever they pleased to him. In the same way the Son of Man is going to suffer at their hands." Then the disciples understood that he had spoken to them about John the Baptist.

Healing a Demonized Boy

The next day, when they came down from the mountain, they came to the disciples. There was a large crowd around them and scribes disputing with them. When the whole crowd saw him, they were amazed and ran to greet him. He asked them, "What are you arguing with them about?"

Just then a man from the crowd approached and knelt down before him and cried out, "Lord, have mercy on my son because he's my only child. He has seizures and suffers terribly. He has a spirit that makes him unable to speak. Whenever it seizes him, suddenly he shrieks, and it throws him down into convulsions, severely bruising him, and he foams at the mouth, grinds his teeth, and becomes rigid. He often falls into the fire and often into the water. It scarcely ever leaves him. I begged your disciples to drive it out, but they couldn't heal him."

Jesus replied, "You unbelieving and perverse generation, how long will I be with you? How long must I put up with you? Bring him here to me."

So they brought the boy to him. When the spirit saw him, it immediately threw the boy into convulsions. He fell to the ground and rolled around, foaming at the mouth. "How long has this been happening to him?" Jesus asked his father.

"From childhood," he said. "And many times it has thrown him into fire or water to destroy him. But if you can do anything, have compassion on us and help us."

Jesus said to him, "'If you can'? Everything is possible for the one who believes."

Immediately the father of the boy cried out, "I do believe; help my unbelief!"

When Jesus saw that a crowd was quickly gathering, he rebuked the unclean spirit, saying to it, "You mute and deaf spirit, I command you: Come out of him and never enter him again."

Then it came out, shrieking and throwing him into terrible convulsions. The boy became like a corpse, so that many said, "He's dead." But Jesus, taking him by the hand, raised him, and he stood up. The boy was healed and given back to his father. And they were all astonished at the greatness of God.

After he had gone into the house, his disciples asked him privately, "Why couldn't we drive it out?"

And he told them, "Because of your little faith. For truly I tell you, if you have faith the size of a mustard seed, you will tell this mountain, 'Move from here to there,' and it will move. Nothing will be impossible for you. This kind can come out by nothing but prayer."

DAY
EIGHTEEN

Predicting His Death

Then they left that place and made their way through Galilee, but he did not want anyone to know it. For he was teaching his disciples and telling them, "The Son of Man is going to be betrayed into the hands of men. They will kill him, and after he is killed, he will rise three days later." But they did not understand this statement; it was concealed from them so that they could not grasp it and were afraid to ask him. They were deeply distressed.

Who Pays the Temple Tax?

When they came to Capernaum, those who collected the temple tax approached Peter and said, "Doesn't your teacher pay the temple tax?"

"Yes," he said.

When he went into the house, Jesus spoke to him first, "What do you think, Simon? From whom do earthly kings collect tariffs or taxes? From their sons or from strangers?"

"From strangers," he said.

"Then the sons are free," Jesus told him. "But, so we won't offend them, go to the sea, cast in a fishhook, and take the first fish that you catch. When you open its mouth you'll find a coin. Take it and give it to them for me and you."

Who Is the Greatest?

They came to Capernaum. When he was in the house, he asked them, "What were you arguing about on the way?" But they were silent, because on the way they had been arguing with one another about who was the greatest. Sitting down, knowing their inner thoughts, he called the Twelve and said to them, "If anyone wants to be first, he must be last and servant of all."

He called a small child and had him stand among them and took him in his arms. "Truly I tell you," he said, "unless you turn and become like little children, you will never enter the kingdom of heaven. Therefore, whoever humbles himself like this child—this one is the greatest in the kingdom of heaven."

He told them, "Whoever welcomes one child like this in my name welcomes me. And whoever welcomes me welcomes him who sent me. For whoever is least among you—this one is great."

John said to him, "Teacher, we saw someone driving out demons in your name, and we tried to stop him because he wasn't following us."

"Don't stop him," said Jesus, "because there is no one who will perform a miracle in my name who can soon afterward speak evil of me. For whoever is not against us is for us. And whoever gives you a cup of water to drink in my name, because you belong to Christ—truly I tell you, he will never lose his reward.

"But whoever causes one of these little ones who believe in me to fall away—it would be better for him if a heavy millstone were hung around his neck and he were drowned in the depths of the sea. Woe to the world because of offenses. For offenses will inevitably come, but woe to that person by whom the offense comes. If your hand or your foot causes you to fall away, cut it off and throw it away. It is better for you to enter life maimed or lame than to have two hands or two feet and be thrown into hell, the unquenchable fire. And if your eye causes you to fall away, gouge it out and throw it away. It is better for you to enter life with one eye than to have two eyes and be thrown into hell where 'their worm does not die, and the fire is not quenched.' For everyone will be salted with fire. Salt is good, but if the salt should lose its flavor, how can you season it? Have salt among yourselves, and be at peace with one another.

"See to it that you don't despise one of these little ones, because I tell you that in heaven their angels continually view the face of my Father in heaven."

Restoring Broken Relationships

"If your brother sins against you, go tell him his fault, between you and him alone. If he listens to you, you have won your brother. But if he won't listen, take one or two others with you, so that 'by the testimony of two or three witnesses every fact may be established.' If he doesn't pay attention to them, tell the church. If he doesn't pay attention even to the church, let him be like a Gentile and a tax collector to you. Truly I tell you, whatever you bind on earth will have been bound in heaven, and whatever you loose on earth will have been loosed in heaven. Again, truly I tell you, if two of you on earth agree about any matter that you pray for, it will be done for you by my Father in heaven. For where two or three are gathered together in my name, I am there among them."

Forgiveness without Limit

Then Peter approached him and asked, "Lord, how many times must I forgive my brother or sister who sins against me? As many as seven times?"

"I tell you, not as many as seven," Jesus replied, "but seventy times seven."

"For this reason, the kingdom of heaven can be compared to a king who wanted to settle accounts with his servants. When he began to settle accounts, one who owed ten thousand talents was brought before him. Since he did not have the money to pay it back, his master commanded that he, his wife, his children, and everything he had be sold to pay the debt.

"At this, the servant fell facedown before him and said, 'Be patient with me, and I will pay you everything.' Then the master of that servant had compassion, released him, and forgave him the loan.

"That servant went out and found one of his fellow servants who owed him a hundred denarii. He grabbed him, started choking him, and said, 'Pay what you owe!'

"At this, his fellow servant fell down and began begging him, 'Be patient with me, and I will pay you back.' But he wasn't willing. Instead, he went and threw him into prison until he could pay what was owed. When the other servants saw what had taken place, they were deeply distressed and went and reported to their master everything that had happened. Then, after he had summoned him, his master said to him, 'You wicked servant! I forgave you all that debt because you begged me. Shouldn't you also have had mercy on your fellow servant, as I had mercy on you?' And because he was angry, his master handed him over to the jailers to be tortured until he could pay everything that was owed. So also my heavenly Father will do to you unless every one of you forgives his brother or sister from your heart."

Journey through Samaria

When the days were coming to a close for him to be taken up, he determined to journey to Jerusalem. He sent messengers ahead of himself, and on the way they entered a village of the Samaritans to make preparations for him. But they did not welcome him, because he determined to journey to Jerusalem. When the disciples James and John saw this, they said, "Lord, do you want us to call down fire from heaven to consume them?"

But he turned and rebuked them, and they went to another village.

The Cost of Following Jesus

As they were traveling on the road a scribe approached and said to him, "Teacher, I will follow you wherever you go."

Jesus told him, "Foxes have dens, and birds of the sky have nests, but the Son of Man has no place to lay his head." Then he said to another disciple, "Follow me."

"Lord," he said, "first let me go bury my father."

But he told him, "Follow me, and let the dead bury their own dead, but you go and spread the news of the kingdom of God."

Another said, "I will follow you, Lord, but first let me go and say good-bye to those at my house."

But Jesus said to him, "No one who puts his hand to the plow and looks back is fit for the kingdom of God."

DAY NINETEEN

Jesus Arrives at the Festival and Begins Teaching

After his brothers had gone up to the festival, then he also went up, not openly but secretly. The Jews were looking for him at the festival and saying, "Where is he?" And there was a lot of murmuring about him among the crowds. Some were saying, "He's a good man." Others were saying, "No, on the contrary, he's deceiving the people." Still, nobody was talking publicly about him for fear of the Jews.

When the festival was already half over, Jesus went up into the temple and began to teach. Then the Jews were amazed and said, "How is this man so learned, since he hasn't been trained?"

Jesus answered them, "My teaching isn't mine but is from the one who sent me. If anyone wants to do his will, he will know whether the teaching is from God or whether I am speaking on my own. The one who speaks on his own seeks his own glory; but he who seeks the glory of the one who sent him is true, and there is no unrighteousness in him. Didn't Moses give you the law? Yet none of you keeps the law. Why are you trying to kill me?"

"You have a demon!" the crowd responded. "Who is trying to kill you?"

"I performed one work, and you are all amazed," Jesus answered. "This is why Moses has given you circumcision—not that it comes from Moses but from the fathers—and you circumcise a man on the Sabbath. If a man receives circumcision on the Sabbath so that the law of Moses won't be broken, are you angry at me because I made a man entirely well on the Sabbath? Stop judging according to outward appearances; rather judge according to righteous judgment."

Some of the people of Jerusalem were saying, "Isn't this the man they are trying to kill? Yet, look, he's speaking publicly and they're saying nothing to him. Can it be true that the authorities know he is the Messiah? But we know where this man is from. When the Messiah comes, nobody will know where he is from."

As he was teaching in the temple, Jesus cried out, "You know me and you know where I am from. Yet I have not come on my own, but the one who sent me is true. You don't know him; I know him because I am from him, and he sent me."

Then they tried to seize him. Yet no one laid a hand on him because his hour had not yet come. However, many from the crowd believed in him and said, "When the Messiah comes, he won't perform more signs than this man has done, will he?"

The Pharisees heard the crowd murmuring these things about him, and so the chief priests and the Pharisees sent servants to arrest him.

Then Jesus said, "I am only with you for a short time. Then I'm going to the one who sent me. You will look for me, but you will not find me; and where I am, you cannot come."

Then the Jews said to one another, "Where does he intend to go that we won't find him? He doesn't intend to go to the Jewish people dispersed among the Greeks and teach the Greeks, does he? What is this remark he made: 'You will look for me, and you will not find me; and where I am, you cannot come'?"

Streams of Living Water

On the last and most important day of the festival, Jesus stood up and cried out, "If anyone is thirsty, let him come to me and drink. The one who believes in me, as the Scripture has said, will have streams of living water flow from deep within him." He said this about the Spirit. Those who believed in Jesus were going to receive the Spirit, for the Spirit had not yet been given because Jesus had not yet been glorified.

When some from the crowd heard these words, they said, "This truly is the Prophet." Others said, "This is the Messiah." But some said, "Surely the Messiah doesn't come from Galilee, does he? Doesn't the Scripture say that the Messiah comes from David's offspring and from the town of Bethlehem, where David lived?" So the crowd was divided because of him. Some of them wanted to seize him, but no one laid hands on him.

Then the servants came to the chief priests and Pharisees, who asked them, "Why didn't you bring him?"

The servants answered, "No man ever spoke like this!"

Then the Pharisees responded to them, "Are you fooled too? Have any of the rulers or Pharisees believed in him? But this crowd, which doesn't know the law, is accursed."

Nicodemus—the one who came to him previously and who was one of them—said to them, "Our law doesn't judge a man before it hears from him and knows what he's doing, does it?"

"You aren't from Galilee too, are you?" they replied. "Investigate and you will see that no prophet arises from Galilee."

Then each one went to his house. But Jesus went to the Mount of Olives.

A Woman Caught in Adultery

At dawn he went to the temple again, and all the people were coming to him. He sat down and began to teach them.

Then the scribes and the Pharisees brought a woman caught in adultery, making her stand in the center. "Teacher," they said to him, "this woman was caught in the act of committing adultery. In the law Moses commanded us to stone such women. So what do you say?" They asked this to trap him, in order that they might have evidence to accuse him.

Jesus stooped down and started writing on the ground with his finger. When they persisted in questioning him, he stood up and said to them, "The one without sin among you should be the first to throw a stone at her." Then he stooped down again and continued writing on the ground. When they heard this, they left one by one, starting with the older men. Only he was left, with the woman in the center. When Jesus stood up, he said to her, "Woman, where are they? Has no one condemned you?"

"No one, Lord," she answered.

"Neither do I condemn you," said Jesus. "Go, and from now on do not sin anymore."

The Light of the World

Jesus spoke to them again: "I am the light of the world. Anyone who follows me will never walk in the darkness but will have the light of life."

So the Pharisees said to him, "You are testifying about yourself. Your testimony is not valid."

"Even if I testify about myself," Jesus replied, "My testimony is true, because I know where I came from and where I'm going. But you don't know where I come from or where I'm going. You judge by human standards. I judge no one. And if I do judge, my judgment is true, because it is not I alone who judge, but I and the Father who sent me. Even in your law it is written that the testimony of two witnesses is true. I am the one who testifies about myself, and the Father who sent me testifies about me."

Then they asked him, "Where is your Father?"

"You know neither me nor my Father," Jesus answered. "If you knew me, you would also know my Father." He spoke these words by the treasury, while teaching in the temple. But no one seized him, because his hour had not yet come.

Then he said to them again, "I'm going away; you will look for me, and you will die in your sin. Where I'm going, you cannot come."

So the Jews said again, "He won't kill himself, will he, since he says, 'Where I'm going, you cannot come'?"

"You are from below," he told them, "I am from above. You are of this world; I am not of this world. Therefore I told you that you will die in your sins. For if you do not believe that I am he, you will die in your sins."

"Who are you?" they questioned.

"Exactly what I've been telling you from the very beginning," Jesus told them. "I have many things to say and to judge about you, but the one who sent me is true, and what I have heard from him—these things I tell the world."

They did not know he was speaking to them about the Father. So Jesus said to them, "When you lift up the Son of Man, then you will know that I am he, and that I do nothing on my own. But just as the Father taught me, I say these things. The one who sent me is with me. He has not left me alone, because I always do what pleases him."

As he was saying these things, many believed in him.

DAY TWENTY

The Truth Will Set You Free

Then Jesus said to the Jews who had believed him, "If you continue in my word, you really are my disciples. You will know the truth, and the truth will set you free."

"We are descendants of Abraham," they answered him, "and we have never been enslaved to anyone. How can you say, 'You will become free'?"

Jesus responded, "Truly I tell you, everyone who commits sin is a slave of sin. A slave does not remain in the household forever, but a son does remain forever. So if the Son sets you free, you really will be free. I know you are descendants of Abraham, but you are trying to kill me because my word has no place among you. I speak what I have seen in the presence of the Father; so then, you do what you have heard from your father."

"Our father is Abraham," they replied.

"If you were Abraham's children," Jesus told them, "you would do what Abraham did. But now you are trying to kill me, a man who has told you the truth that I heard from God. Abraham did not do this. You're doing what your father does."

"We weren't born of sexual immorality," they said. "We have one Father—God."

Jesus said to them, "If God were your Father, you would love me, because I came from God and I am here. For I didn't come on my own, but he sent me. Why don't you understand what I say? Because you cannot listen to my word. You are of your father the devil, and you want to carry out your father's desires. He was a murderer from the beginning and does not stand in the truth, because there is no truth in him. When he tells a lie, he speaks from his own nature, because he is a liar and the father of lies. Yet because I tell the truth, you do not believe me. Who among you can convict me of sin? If I am telling the truth, why don't you believe me? The one who is from God listens to God's words. This is why you don't listen, because you are not from God."

The Jews responded to him, "Aren't we right in saying that you're a Samaritan and have a demon?"

"I do not have a demon," Jesus answered. "On the contrary, I honor my Father and you dishonor me. I do not seek my own glory; there is one who seeks it and judges. Truly I tell you, if anyone keeps my word, he will never see death."

Then the Jews said, "Now we know you have a demon. Abraham died and so did the prophets. You say, 'If anyone keeps my word, he will never taste death.' Are you greater than our father Abraham who died? And the prophets died. Who do you claim to be?"

"If I glorify myself," Jesus answered, "my glory is nothing. My Father—about whom you say, 'He is our God'—he is the one who glorifies me. You do not know him, but I know him. If I were to say I don't know him, I would be a liar like you. But I do know him, and I keep his word. Your father Abraham rejoiced to see my day; he saw it and was glad."

The Jews replied, "You aren't fifty years old yet, and you've seen Abraham?"

Jesus said to them, "Truly I tell you, before Abraham was, I am."

So they picked up stones to throw at him. But Jesus was hidden and went out of the temple.

Jesus Sends Seventy-Two Disciples

After this, the Lord appointed seventy-two others, and he sent them ahead of him in pairs to every town and place where he himself was about to go. He told them, "The harvest is abundant, but the workers are few. Therefore, pray to the Lord of the harvest to send out workers into his harvest. Now go; I'm sending you out like lambs among wolves. Don't carry a money-bag, traveling bag, or sandals; don't greet anyone along the road. Whatever house you enter, first say, 'Peace to this household.' If a person of peace is there, your peace will rest on him; but if not, it will return to you. Remain in the same house, eating and drinking what they offer, for the worker is worthy of his wages. Don't move from house to house. When you enter any town, and they welcome you, eat the things set before you. Heal the sick who are there, and tell them, 'The kingdom of God has come near you.' When you enter any town, and they don't welcome you, go out into its streets and say, 'We are wiping off even the dust of your town that clings to our feet as a witness against you. Know this for certain: The kingdom of God has come near.' I tell you, on that day it will be more tolerable for Sodom than for that town.

"Woe to you, Chorazin! Woe to you, Bethsaida! For if the miracles that were done in you had been done in Tyre and Sidon, they would have repented long ago, sitting in sackcloth and ashes. But it will be more tolerable for Tyre and Sidon at the judgment than for you. And you, Capernaum, will you be exalted to heaven? No, you will go down to Hades. Whoever listens to you listens to me. Whoever rejects you rejects me. And whoever rejects me rejects the one who sent me."

The seventy-two returned with joy, saying, "Lord, even the demons submit to us in your name."

He said to them, "I watched Satan fall from heaven like lightning. Look, I have given you the authority to trample on snakes and scorpions and over all the power of the enemy; nothing at all will harm you. However, don't rejoice that the spirits submit to you, but rejoice that your names are written in heaven."

At that time he rejoiced in the Holy Spirit and said, "I praise you, Father, Lord of heaven and earth, because you have hidden these things from the wise and intelligent and revealed them to infants. Yes, Father, because this was your good pleasure. All things have been entrusted to me by my Father. No one knows who the Son is except the Father, and who the Father is except the Son, and anyone to whom the Son desires to reveal him."

Then turning to his disciples he said privately, "Blessed are the eyes that see the things you see! For I tell you that many prophets and kings wanted to see the things you see but didn't see them; to hear the things you hear but didn't hear them."

The Good Samaritan

Then an expert in the law stood up to test him, saying, "Teacher, what must I do to inherit eternal life?"

"What is written in the law?" he asked him. "How do you read it?"

He answered, "Love the Lord your God with all your heart, with all your soul, with all your strength, and with all your mind," and "your neighbor as yourself."

"You've answered correctly," he told him. "Do this and you will live."

But wanting to justify himself, he asked Jesus, "And who is my neighbor?"

Jesus took up the question and said, "A man was going down from Jerusalem to Jericho and fell into the hands of robbers. They stripped him, beat him up, and fled, leaving him half dead. A priest happened to be going down that road. When he saw him, he passed by on the other side. In the same way, a Levite, when he arrived at the place and saw him, passed by on the other side. But a Samaritan on his journey came up to him, and when he saw the man, he had compassion. He went over to him and bandaged his wounds, pouring on olive oil and wine. Then he put him on his own animal, brought him to an inn, and took care of him. The next day he took out two denarii, gave them to the innkeeper, and said, 'Take care of him. When I come back I'll reimburse you for whatever extra you spend.'

"Which of these three do you think proved to be a neighbor to the man who fell into the hands of the robbers?"

"The one who showed mercy to him," he said.

Then Jesus told him, "Go and do the same."

Jesus Visits Mary and Martha

While they were traveling, he entered a village, and a woman named Martha welcomed him into her home. She had a sister named Mary, who also sat at the Lord's feet and was listening to what he said. But Martha was distracted by her many tasks, and she came up and asked, "Lord, don't you care that my sister has left me to serve alone? So tell her to give me a hand."

The Lord answered her, "Martha, Martha, you are worried and upset about many things, but one thing is necessary. Mary has made the right choice, and it will not be taken away from her."

DAY
TWENTY-ONE

The Way to Pray

He was praying in a certain place, and when he finished, one of his disciples said to him, "Lord, teach us to pray, just as John also taught his disciples."

He said to them, "Whenever you pray, say,

Father,
your name be honored as holy.
Your kingdom come.
Give us each day our daily bread.
And forgive us our sins,
for we ourselves also forgive everyone
in debt to us.
And do not bring us into temptation."

He also said to them, "Suppose one of you has a friend and goes to him at midnight and says to him, 'Friend, lend me three loaves of bread, because a friend of mine on a journey has come to me, and I don't have anything to offer him.' Then he will answer from inside and say, 'Don't bother me! The door is already locked, and my children and I have gone to bed. I can't get up to give you anything.' I tell you, even though he won't get up and give him anything because he is his friend, yet because of his friend's shameless boldness he will get up and give him as much as he needs.

"So I say to you, ask, and it will be given to you. Seek, and you will find. Knock, and the door will be opened to you. For everyone who asks receives, and the one who seeks finds, and to the one who knocks, the door will be opened. What father among you, if his son asks for a fish, will give him a snake instead of a fish? Or if he asks for an egg, will give him a scorpion? If you then, who are evil, know how to give good gifts to your children, how much more will the heavenly Father give the Holy Spirit to those who ask him?"

Blasphemous Accusations

Jesus entered a house, and the crowd gathered again so that they were not even able to eat. When his family heard this, they set out to restrain him, because they said, "He's out of his mind."

Then a demon-possessed man who was blind and unable to speak was brought to him. He healed him, so that the man could both speak and see. All the crowds were astounded and said, "Could this be the Son of David?"

When the Pharisees and scribes who had come down from Jerusalem heard this, they said, "This man drives out demons only by Beelzebul, the ruler of the demons." And others, as a test, were demanding of him a sign from heaven.

Knowing their thoughts, he summoned them and spoke to them in parables: "Every kingdom divided against itself is headed for destruction, and no city or house divided against itself will stand. If Satan drives out Satan, he is divided against himself. How then will his kingdom stand? And if I drive out demons by Beelzebul, by whom do your sons drive them out? For this reason they will be your judges. If I drive out demons by the Spirit of God, then the kingdom of God has come upon you. When a strong man, fully armed, guards his estate, his possessions are secure. But when one stronger than he attacks and overpowers him, he takes from him all his weapons he trusted in, and then he can plunder his house. Anyone who is not with me is against me, and anyone who does not gather with me scatters. Therefore, I tell you, people will be forgiven every sin and blasphemy, but the blasphemy against the Spirit will not be forgiven but is guilty of an eternal sin. Whoever speaks a word against the Son of Man, it will be forgiven him; but whoever speaks against the Holy Spirit, it will not be forgiven him, either in this age or in the one to come"—because they were saying, "He has an unclean spirit."

"Either make the tree good and its fruit will be good, or make the tree bad and its fruit will be bad; for a tree is known by its fruit. Brood of vipers! How can you speak good things when you are evil? For the mouth speaks from the overflow of the heart. A good person produces good things from his storeroom of good, and an evil person produces evil things from his storeroom of evil. I tell you that on the day of judgment people will have to account for every careless word they speak. For by your words you will be acquitted, and by your words you will be condemned."

The Sign of Jonah

Then some of the scribes and Pharisees said to him, "Teacher, we want to see a sign from you."

He answered them, "An evil and adulterous generation demands a sign, but no sign will be given to it except the sign of the prophet Jonah. For as Jonah was in the belly of the huge fish three days and three nights, so the Son of Man will be in the heart of the earth three days and three nights. The men of Nineveh will stand up at the judgment with this generation and condemn it, because they repented at Jonah's preaching; and look—something greater than Jonah is here. The queen of the south will rise up at the judgment with this generation and condemn it, because she came from the ends of the earth to hear the wisdom of Solomon; and look—something greater than Solomon is here.

"When an unclean spirit comes out of a person, it roams through waterless places looking for rest but doesn't find any. Then it says, 'I'll go back to my house that I came from.' Returning, it finds the house vacant, swept, and put in order. Then it goes and brings with it seven other spirits more evil than itself, and they enter and settle down there. As a result, that person's last condition is worse than the first. That's how it will also be with this evil generation.

"No one lights a lamp and puts it in the cellar or under a basket, but on a lampstand, so that those who come in may see its light. Your eye is the lamp of the body. When your eye is healthy, your whole body is also full of light. But when it is bad, your body is also full of darkness. Take care, then, that the light in you is not darkness. If, therefore, your whole body is full of light, with no part of it in darkness, it will be entirely illuminated, as when a lamp shines its light on you."

As he was saying these things, a woman from the crowd raised her voice and said to him, "Blessed is the womb that bore you and the one who nursed you!"

He said, "Rather, blessed are those who hear the word of God and keep it."

Woe to the Pharisees

As he was speaking, a Pharisee asked him to dine with him. So he went in and reclined at the table. When the Pharisee saw this, he was amazed that he did not first perform the ritual washing before dinner. But the Lord said to him, "Now you Pharisees clean the outside of the cup and dish, but inside you are full of greed and evil. Fools! Didn't he who made the outside make the inside too? But give from what is within to the poor, and then everything is clean for you.

"But woe to you Pharisees! You give a tenth of mint, rue, and every kind of herb, and you bypass justice and love for God. These things you should have done without neglecting the others.

"Woe to you Pharisees! You love the front seat in the synagogues and greetings in the marketplaces.

"Woe to you! You are like unmarked graves; the people who walk over them don't know it."

One of the experts in the law answered him, "Teacher, when you say these things you insult us too."

Then he said, "Woe also to you experts in the law! You load people with burdens that are hard to carry, and yet you yourselves don't touch these burdens with one of your fingers.

"Woe to you! You build tombs for the prophets, and your fathers killed them. Therefore, you are witnesses that you approve the deeds of your fathers, for they killed them, and you build their monuments. Because of this, the wisdom of God said, 'I will send them prophets and apostles, and some of them they will kill and persecute,' so that this generation may be held responsible for the blood of all the prophets shed since the foundation of the world—from the blood of Abel to the blood of Zechariah, who perished between the altar and the sanctuary.

"Yes, I tell you, this generation will be held responsible.

"Woe to you experts in the law! You have taken away the key to knowledge. You didn't go in yourselves, and you hindered those who were trying to go in."

When he left there, the scribes and the Pharisees began to oppose him fiercely and to cross-examine him about many things; they were lying in wait for him to trap him in something he said.

DAY
TWENTY-TWO

A Warning about Hypocrisy

Meanwhile, a crowd of many thousands came together, so that they were trampling on one another. He began to say to his disciples first, "Be on your guard against the leaven of the Pharisees, which is hypocrisy. There is nothing covered that won't be uncovered, nothing hidden that won't be made known. Therefore, whatever you have said in the dark will be heard in the light, and what you have whispered in an ear in private rooms will be proclaimed on the housetops.

"I say to you, my friends, don't fear those who kill the body, and after that can do nothing more. But I will show you the one to fear: Fear him who has authority to throw people into hell after death. Yes, I say to you, this is the one to fear! Aren't five sparrows sold for two pennies? Yet not one of them is forgotten in God's sight. Indeed, the hairs of your head are all counted. Don't be afraid; you are worth more than many sparrows.

"And I say to you, anyone who acknowledges me before others, the Son of Man will also acknowledge him before the angels of God, but whoever denies me before others will be denied before the angels of God.

Anyone who speaks a word against the Son of Man will be forgiven, but the one who blasphemes against the Holy Spirit will not be forgiven. Whenever they bring you before synagogues and rulers and authorities, don't worry about how you should defend yourselves or what you should say. For the Holy Spirit will teach you at that very hour what must be said."

A Warning about Possessions and Worry

Someone from the crowd said to him, "Teacher, tell my brother to divide the inheritance with me."

"Friend," he said to him, "who appointed me a judge or arbitrator over you?" He then told them, "Watch out and be on guard against all greed, because one's life is not in the abundance of his possessions."

Then he told them a parable: "A rich man's land was very productive. He thought to himself, 'What should I do, since I don't have anywhere to store my crops? I will do this,' he said. 'I'll tear down my barns and build bigger ones and store all my grain and my goods there. Then I'll say to myself, 'You have many goods stored up for many years. Take it easy; eat, drink, and enjoy yourself.'

"But God said to him, 'You fool! This very night your life is demanded of you. And the things you have prepared—whose will they be?'

"That's how it is with the one who stores up treasure for himself and is not rich toward God."

Then he said to his disciples, "Therefore I tell you, don't worry about your life, what you will eat; or about the body, what you will wear. For life is more than food and the body more than clothing. Consider the ravens: They don't sow or reap; they don't have a storeroom or a barn; yet God feeds them. Aren't you worth much more than the birds? Can any of you add one moment to his life span by worrying? If then you're not able to do even a little thing, why worry about the rest?

"Consider how the wildflowers grow: They don't labor or spin thread. Yet I tell you, not even Solomon in all his splendor was adorned like one of these. If that's how God clothes the grass, which is in the field today and is thrown into the furnace tomorrow, how much more will he do for you—you of little faith? Don't strive for what you should eat and what you should drink, and don't be anxious. For the Gentile world eagerly seeks all these things, and your Father knows that you need them.

"But seek his kingdom, and these things will be provided for you. Don't be afraid, little flock, because your Father delights to give you the kingdom. Sell your possessions and give to the poor. Make money-bags for yourselves that won't grow old, an inexhaustible treasure in heaven, where no thief comes near and no moth destroys. For where your treasure is, there your heart will be also."

Always Be Ready

"Be ready for service and have your lamps lit. You are to be like people waiting for their master to return from the wedding banquet so that when he comes and knocks, they can open the door for him at once. Blessed will be those servants the master finds alert when he comes. Truly I tell you, he will get ready, have them recline at the table, then come and serve them. If he comes in the middle of the night, or even near dawn, and finds them alert, blessed are those servants. But know this: If the homeowner had known at what hour the thief was coming, he would not have let his house be broken into. You also be ready, because the Son of Man is coming at an hour you do not expect."

"Lord," Peter asked, "are you telling this parable to us or to everyone?"

The Lord said, "Who then is the faithful and sensible manager his master will put in charge of his household servants to give them their allotted food at the proper time? Blessed is that servant whom the master finds doing his job when he comes. Truly I tell you, he will put him in charge of all his possessions. But if that servant says in his heart, 'My master is delaying his coming,' and starts to beat the male and female servants, and to eat and drink and get drunk, that servant's master will come on a day he does not expect him and at an hour he does not know. He will cut him to pieces and assign him a place with the unfaithful. And that servant who knew his master's will and didn't prepare himself or do it will be severely beaten. But the one who did not know and did what deserved punishment will receive a light beating. From everyone who has been given much, much will be required; and from the one who has been entrusted with much, even more will be expected."

A Warning about the Signs of the Times

"I came to bring fire on the earth, and how I wish it were already set ablaze! But I have a baptism to undergo, and how it consumes me until it is finished! Do you think that I came here to bring peace on the earth? No, I tell you, but rather division. From now on, five in one household will be divided: three against two, and two against three.

> They will be divided, father against son,
> son against father,
> mother against daughter,
> daughter against mother,
> mother-in-law against her daughter-in-law,
> and daughter-in-law against mother-in-law."

He also said to the crowds, "When you see a cloud rising in the west, right away you say, 'A storm is coming,' and so it does. And when the south wind is blowing, you say, 'It's going to be hot,' and it is. Hypocrites! You know how to interpret the appearance of the earth and the sky, but why don't you know how to interpret this present time?

"Why don't you judge for yourselves what is right? As you are going with your adversary to the ruler, make an effort to settle with him on the way. Then he won't drag you before the judge, the judge hand you over to the bailiff, and the bailiff throw you into prison. I tell you, you will never get out of there until you have paid the last penny."

Repent or Perish

At that time, some people came and reported to him about the Galileans whose blood Pilate had mixed with their sacrifices. And he responded to them, "Do you think that these Galileans were more sinful than all the other Galileans because they suffered these things? No, I tell you; but unless you repent, you will all perish as well. Or those eighteen that the tower in Siloam fell on and killed—do you think they were more sinful than all the other people who live in Jerusalem? No, I tell you; but unless you repent, you will all perish as well."

And he told this parable: "A man had a fig tree that was planted in his vineyard. He came looking for fruit on it and found none. He told the vineyard worker, 'Listen, for three years I have come looking for fruit on this fig tree and haven't found any. Cut it down! Why should it even waste the soil?'

"But he replied to him, 'Sir, leave it this year also, until I dig around it and fertilize it. Perhaps it will produce fruit next year, but if not, you can cut it down.'"

DAY
TWENTY-THREE

Jesus Heals a Crippled Woman

As he was teaching in one of the synagogues on the Sabbath, a woman was there who had been disabled by a spirit for over eighteen years. She was bent over and could not straighten up at all. When Jesus saw her, he called out to her, "Woman, you are free of your disability." Then he laid his hands on her, and instantly she was restored and began to glorify God.

But the leader of the synagogue, indignant because Jesus had healed on the Sabbath, responded by telling the crowd, "There are six days when work should be done; therefore come on those days and be healed and not on the Sabbath day."

But the Lord answered him and said, "Hypocrites! Doesn't each one of you untie his ox or donkey from the feeding trough on the Sabbath and lead it to water? Satan has bound this woman, a daughter of Abraham, for eighteen years—shouldn't she be untied from this bondage on the Sabbath day?"

When he had said these things, all his adversaries were humiliated, but the whole crowd was rejoicing over all the glorious things he was doing.

He said, therefore, "What is the kingdom of God like, and what can I compare it to? It's like a mustard seed that a man took and sowed in his garden. It grew and became a tree, and the birds of the sky nested in its branches."

Again he said, "What can I compare the kingdom of God to? It's like leaven that a woman took and mixed into fifty pounds of flour until all of it was leavened."

A Man Born Blind

As he was passing by, he saw a man blind from birth. His disciples asked him, "Rabbi, who sinned, this man or his parents, that he was born blind?"

"Neither this man nor his parents sinned," Jesus answered. "This came about so that God's works might be displayed in him. We must do the works of him who sent me while it is day. Night is coming when no one can work. As long as I am in the world, I am the light of the world."

After he said these things he spit on the ground, made some mud from the saliva, and spread the mud on his eyes. "Go," he told him, "wash in the pool of Siloam" (which means "Sent"). So he left, washed, and came back seeing.

Blind Man Questioned after Healing

His neighbors and those who had seen him before as a beggar said, "Isn't this the one who used to sit begging?"

Some said, "He's the one." Others were saying, "No, but he looks like him."

He kept saying, "I'm the one."

So they asked him, "Then how were your eyes opened?"

He answered, "The man called Jesus made mud, spread it on my eyes, and told me, 'Go to Siloam and wash.' So when I went and washed I received my sight."

"Where is he?" they asked.

"I don't know," he said.

They brought the man who used to be blind to the Pharisees. The day that Jesus made the mud and opened his eyes was a Sabbath. Then the Pharisees asked him again how he received his sight.

"He put mud on my eyes," he told them. "I washed and I can see."

Some of the Pharisees said, "This man is not from God, because he doesn't keep the Sabbath." But others were saying, "How can a sinful man perform such signs?" And there was a division among them.

Again they asked the blind man, "What do you say about him, since he opened your eyes?"

"He's a prophet," he said.

The Jews did not believe this about him—that he was blind and received sight—until they summoned the parents of the one who had received his sight.

They asked them, "Is this your son, the one you say was born blind? How then does he now see?"

"We know this is our son and that he was born blind," his parents answered. "But we don't know how he now sees, and we don't know who opened his eyes. Ask him; he's of age. He will speak for himself." His parents said these things because they were afraid of the Jews, since the Jews had already agreed that if anyone confessed him as the Messiah, he would be banned from the synagogue. This is why his parents said, "He's of age; ask him."

So a second time they summoned the man who had been blind and told him, "Give glory to God. We know that this man is a sinner."

He answered, "Whether or not he's a sinner, I don't know. One thing I do know: I was blind, and now I can see!"

Then they asked him, "What did he do to you? How did he open your eyes?"

"I already told you," he said, "and you didn't listen. Why do you want to hear it again? You don't want to become his disciples too, do you?"

They ridiculed him: "You're that man's disciple, but we're Moses's disciples. We know that God has spoken to Moses. But this man—we don't know where he's from."

"This is an amazing thing!" the man told them. "You don't know where he is from, and yet he opened my eyes. We know that God doesn't listen to sinners, but if anyone is God-fearing and does his will, he listens to him. Throughout history no one has ever heard of someone opening the eyes of a person born blind. If this man were not from God, he wouldn't be able to do anything."

"You were born entirely in sin," they replied, "and are you trying to teach us?" Then they threw him out.

Spiritual Blindness

Jesus heard that they had thrown the man out, and when he found him, he asked, "Do you believe in the Son of Man?"

"Who is he, Sir, that I may believe in him?" he asked.

Jesus answered, "You have seen him; in fact, he is the one speaking with you."

"I believe, Lord!" he said, and he worshiped him.

Jesus said, "I came into this world for judgment, in order that those who do not see will see and those who do see will become blind."

Some of the Pharisees who were with him heard these things and asked him, "We aren't blind too, are we?"

"If you were blind," Jesus told them, "you wouldn't have sin. But now that you say, 'We see,' your sin remains.

The Good Shepherd

"Truly I tell you, anyone who doesn't enter the sheep pen by the gate but climbs in some other way is a thief and a robber. The one who enters by the gate is the shepherd of the sheep. The gatekeeper opens it for him, and the sheep hear his voice. He calls his own sheep by name and leads them out. When he has brought all his own outside, he goes ahead of them. The sheep follow him because they know his voice. They will never follow a stranger; instead they will run away from him, because they don't know the voice of strangers." Jesus gave them this figure of speech, but they did not understand what he was telling them.

Jesus said again, "Truly I tell you, I am the gate for the sheep. All who came before me are thieves and robbers, but the sheep didn't listen to them. I am the gate. If anyone enters by me, he will be saved and will come in and go out and find pasture. A thief comes only to steal and kill and destroy. I have come so that they may have life and have it in abundance.

"I am the good shepherd. The good shepherd lays down his life for the sheep. The hired hand, since he is not the shepherd and doesn't own the sheep, leaves them and runs away when he sees a wolf coming. The wolf then snatches and scatters them. This happens because he is a hired hand and doesn't care about the sheep.

"I am the good shepherd. I know my own, and my own know me, just as the Father knows me, and I know the Father. I lay down my life for the sheep. But I have other sheep that are not from this sheep pen; I must bring them also, and they will listen to my voice. Then there will be one flock, one shepherd. This is why the Father loves me, because I lay down my life so that I may take it up again. No one takes it from me, but I lay it down on my own. I have the right to lay it down, and I have the right to take it up again. I have received this command from my Father."

Again the Jews were divided because of these words. Many of them were saying, "He has a demon and he's crazy. Why do you listen to him?" Others were saying, "These aren't the words of someone who is demon-possessed. Can a demon open the eyes of the blind?"

DAY
TWENTY-FOUR

Jesus Threatened with Stoning

Then the Festival of Dedication took place in Jerusalem, and it was winter. Jesus was walking in the temple in Solomon's Colonnade. The Jews surrounded him and asked, "How long are you going to keep us in suspense? If you are the Messiah, tell us plainly."

"I did tell you and you don't believe," Jesus answered them. "The works that I do in my Father's name testify about me. But you don't believe because you are not of my sheep. My sheep hear my voice, I know them, and they follow me. I give them eternal life, and they will never perish. No one will snatch them out of my hand. My Father, who has given them to me, is greater than all. No one is able to snatch them out of the Father's hand. I and the Father are one."

Again the Jews picked up rocks to stone him.

Jesus replied, "I have shown you many good works from the Father. For which of these works are you stoning me?"

"We aren't stoning you for a good work," the Jews answered, "but for blasphemy, because you—being a man—make yourself God."

Jesus answered them, "Isn't it written in your law, *I said, you are gods*? If he called those to whom the word of God came 'gods'—and the Scripture cannot be broken—do you say, 'You are blaspheming' to the one the Father set apart and sent into the world, because I said: I am the Son of God? If I am not doing my Father's works, don't believe me. But if I am doing them and you don't believe me, believe the works. This way you will know and understand that the Father is in me and I in the Father." Then they were trying again to seize him, but he escaped their grasp.

So he departed again across the Jordan to the place where John had been baptizing earlier, and he remained there. Many came to him and said, "John never did a sign, but everything John said about this man was true." And many believed in him there.

The Narrow Way to the Kingdom

He went through one town and village after another, teaching and making his way to Jerusalem. "Lord," someone asked him, "are only a few people going to be saved?"

He said to them, "Make every effort to enter through the narrow door, because I tell you, many will try to enter and won't be able once the homeowner gets up and shuts the door. Then you will stand outside and knock on the door, saying, 'Lord, open up for us!' He will answer you, 'I don't know you or where you're from.' Then you will say, 'We ate and drank in your presence, and you taught in our streets.' But he will say, 'I tell you, I don't know you or where you're from. Get away from me, all you evildoers!' There will be weeping and gnashing of teeth in that place, when you see Abraham, Isaac, Jacob, and all the prophets in the kingdom of God, but yourselves thrown out. They will come from east and west, from north and south, to share the banquet in the kingdom of God. Note this: Some who are last will be first, and some who are first will be last."

At that time some Pharisees came and told him, "Go, get out of here. Herod wants to kill you."

He said to them, "Go tell that fox, 'Look, I'm driving out demons and performing healings today and tomorrow, and on the third day I will complete my work.' Yet it is necessary that I travel today, tomorrow, and the next day, because it is not possible for a prophet to perish outside of Jerusalem."

Dinner at a Pharisee's House

One Sabbath, when he went in to eat at the house of one of the leading Pharisees, they were watching him closely. There in front of him was a man whose body was swollen with fluid. In response, Jesus asked the law experts and the Pharisees, "Is it lawful to heal on the Sabbath or not?" But they kept silent. He took the man, healed him, and sent him away. And to them, he said, "Which of you whose son or ox falls into a well, will not immediately pull him out on the Sabbath day?" They could find no answer to these things.

He told a parable to those who were invited, when he noticed how they would choose the best places for themselves: "When you are invited by someone to a wedding banquet, don't sit in the place of honor, because a more distinguished person than you may have been invited by your host. The one who invited both of you may come and say to you, 'Give your place to this man,' and then in humiliation, you will proceed to take the lowest place.

"But when you are invited, go and sit in the lowest place, so that when the one who invited you comes, he will say to you, 'Friend, move up higher.' You will then be honored in the presence of all the other guests. For everyone who exalts himself will be humbled, and the one who humbles himself will be exalted."

He also said to the one who had invited him, "When you give a lunch or a dinner, don't invite your friends, your brothers or sisters, your relatives, or your rich neighbors, because they might invite you back, and you would be repaid. On the contrary, when you host a banquet, invite those who are poor, maimed, lame, or blind. And you will be blessed, because they cannot repay you; for you will be repaid at the resurrection of the righteous."

When one of those who reclined at the table with him heard these things, he said to him, "Blessed is the one who will eat bread in the kingdom of God!"

Then he told him, "A man was giving a large banquet and invited many. At the time of the banquet, he sent his servant to tell those who were invited, 'Come, because everything is now ready.'

"But without exception they all began to make excuses. The first one said to him, 'I have bought a field, and I must go out and see it. I ask you to excuse me.'

"Another said, 'I have bought five yoke of oxen, and I'm going to try them out. I ask you to excuse me.'

"And another said, 'I just got married, and therefore I'm unable to come.'

"So the servant came back and reported these things to his master. Then in anger, the master of the house told his servant, 'Go out quickly into the streets and alleys of the city, and bring in here the poor, maimed, blind, and lame.'

"'Master,' the servant said, 'what you ordered has been done, and there's still room.'

"Then the master told the servant, 'Go out into the highways and hedges and make them come in, so that my house may be filled. For I tell you, not one of those people who were invited will enjoy my banquet.'"

The Cost of Discipleship

Now great crowds were traveling with him. So he turned and said to them, "If anyone comes to me and does not hate his own father and mother, wife and children, brothers and sisters—yes, and even his own life—he cannot be my disciple. Whoever does not bear his own cross and come after me cannot be my disciple.

"For which of you, wanting to build a tower, doesn't first sit down and calculate the cost to see if he has enough to complete it? Otherwise, after he has laid the foundation and cannot finish it, all the onlookers will begin to ridicule him, saying, 'This man started to build and wasn't able to finish.'

"Or what king, going to war against another king, will not first sit down and decide if he is able with ten thousand to oppose the one who comes against him with twenty thousand? If not, while the other is still far off, he sends a delegation and asks for terms of peace. In the same way, therefore, every one of you who does not renounce all his possessions cannot be my disciple.

"Now, salt is good, but if salt should lose its taste, how will it be made salty? It isn't fit for the soil or for the manure pile; they throw it out. Let anyone who has ears to hear listen."

Parables of the Lost Sheep and the Lost Coin

All the tax collectors and sinners were approaching to listen to him. And the Pharisees and scribes were complaining, "This man welcomes sinners and eats with them."

So he told them this parable: "What man among you, who has a hundred sheep and loses one of them, does not leave the ninety-nine in the open field and go after the lost one until he finds it? When he has found it, he joyfully puts it on his shoulders, and coming home, he calls his friends and neighbors together, saying to them, 'Rejoice with me, because I have found my lost sheep!' I tell you, in the same way, there will be more joy in heaven over one sinner who repents than over ninety-nine righteous people who don't need repentance.

"Or what woman who has ten silver coins, if she loses one coin, does not light a lamp, sweep the house, and search carefully until she finds it? When she finds it, she calls her friends and neighbors together, saying, 'Rejoice with me, because I have found the silver coin I lost!' I tell you, in the same way, there is joy in the presence of God's angels over one sinner who repents."

DAY
TWENTY-FIVE

Parable of the Prodigal Son

He also said, "A man had two sons. The younger of them said to his father, 'Father, give me the share of the estate I have coming to me.' So he distributed the assets to them. Not many days later, the younger son gathered together all he had and traveled to a distant country, where he squandered his estate in foolish living. After he had spent everything, a severe famine struck that country, and he had nothing. Then he went to work for one of the citizens of that country, who sent him into his fields to feed pigs. He longed to eat his fill from the pods that the pigs were eating, but no one would give him anything. When he came to his senses, he said, 'How many of my father's hired workers have more than enough food, and here I am dying of hunger! I'll get up, go to my father, and say to him, "Father, I have sinned against heaven and in your sight. I'm no longer worthy to be called your son. Make me like one of your hired workers."' So he got up and went to his father. But while the son was still a long way off, his father saw him and was filled with compassion. He ran, threw his arms around his neck, and kissed him. The son said to him, 'Father, I have sinned against heaven and in your sight. I'm no longer worthy to be called your son.'

"But the father told his servants, 'Quick! Bring out the best robe and put it on him; put a ring on his finger and sandals on his feet. Then bring the fattened calf and slaughter it, and let's celebrate with a feast, because this son of mine was dead and is alive again; he was lost and is found!' So they began to celebrate.

"Now his older son was in the field; as he came near the house, he heard music and dancing. So he summoned one of the servants, questioning what these things meant. 'Your brother is here,' he told him, 'and your father has slaughtered the fattened calf because he has him back safe and sound.'

"Then he became angry and didn't want to go in. So his father came out and pleaded with him. But he replied to his father, 'Look, I have been slaving many years for you, and I have never disobeyed your orders, yet you never gave me a goat so that I could celebrate with my friends. But when this son of yours came, who has devoured your assets with prostitutes, you slaughtered the fattened calf for him.'

"'Son,' he said to him, 'you are always with me, and everything I have is yours. But we had to celebrate and rejoice, because this brother of yours was dead and is alive again; he was lost and is found.'"

Parable of the Shrewd Manager

Now he said to the disciples, "There was a rich man who received an accusation that his manager was squandering his possessions. So he called the manager in and asked, 'What is this I hear about you? Give an account of your management, because you can no longer be my manager.'

"Then the manager said to himself, 'What will I do since my master is taking the management away from me? I'm not strong enough to dig; I'm ashamed to beg. I know what I'll do so that when I'm removed from management, people will welcome me into their homes.'

"So he summoned each one of his master's debtors. 'How much do you owe my master?' he asked the first one.

"'A hundred measures of olive oil,' he said.

"'Take your invoice,' he told him, 'sit down quickly, and write fifty.'

"Next he asked another, 'How much do you owe?'

"'A hundred measures of wheat,' he said.

"'Take your invoice,' he told him, 'and write eighty.'

"The master praised the unrighteous manager because he had acted shrewdly. For the children of this age are more shrewd than the children of light in dealing with their own people. And I tell you, make friends for yourselves by means of worldly wealth so that when it fails, they may welcome you into eternal dwellings. Whoever is faithful in very little is also faithful in much, and whoever is unrighteous in very little is also unrighteous in much. So if you have not been faithful with worldly wealth, who will trust you with what is genuine? And if you have not been faithful with what belongs to someone else, who will give you what is your own? No servant can serve two masters, since either he will hate one and love the other, or he will be devoted to one and despise the other. You cannot serve both God and money."

The Danger of Wealth

The Pharisees, who were lovers of money, were listening to all these things and scoffing at him. And he told them, "You are the ones who justify yourselves in the sight of others, but God knows your hearts. For what is highly admired by people is revolting in God's sight.

"The Law and the Prophets were until John; since then, the good news of the kingdom of God has been proclaimed, and everyone is urgently invited to enter it. But it is easier for heaven and earth to pass away than for one stroke of a letter in the law to drop out.

"There was a rich man who would dress in purple and fine linen, feasting lavishly every day. But a poor man named Lazarus, covered with sores, was lying at his gate. He longed to be filled with what fell from the rich man's table, but instead the dogs would come and lick his sores. One day the poor man died and was carried away by the angels to Abraham's side. The rich man also died and was buried. And being in torment in Hades, he looked up and saw Abraham a long way off, with Lazarus at his side. 'Father Abraham!' he called out, 'Have mercy on me and send Lazarus to dip the tip of his finger in water and cool my tongue, because I am in agony in this flame!'

"'Son,' Abraham said, 'remember that during your life you received your good things, just as Lazarus received bad things, but now he is comforted here, while you are in agony. Besides all this, a great chasm has been fixed between us and you, so that those who want to pass over from here to you cannot; neither can those from there cross over to us.'

"'Father,' he said, 'then I beg you to send him to my father's house—because I have five brothers—to warn them, so that they won't also come to this place of torment.'

"But Abraham said, 'They have Moses and the prophets; they should listen to them.'

"'No, father Abraham,' he said. 'But if someone from the dead goes to them, they will repent.'

"But he told him, 'If they don't listen to Moses and the prophets, they will not be persuaded if someone rises from the dead.'"

Lessons on Discipleship

He said to his disciples, "Offenses will certainly come, but woe to the one through whom they come! It would be better for him if a millstone were hung around his neck and he were thrown into the sea than for him to cause one of these little ones to stumble. Be on your guard. If your brother sins, rebuke him, and if he repents, forgive him. And if he sins against you seven times in a day, and comes back to you seven times, saying, 'I repent,' you must forgive him."

The apostles said to the Lord, "Increase our faith."

"If you have faith the size of a mustard seed," the Lord said, "you can say to this mulberry tree, 'Be uprooted and planted in the sea,' and it will obey you.

"Which one of you having a servant tending sheep or plowing will say to him when he comes in from the field, 'Come at once and sit down to eat'? Instead, will he not tell him, 'Prepare something for me to eat, get ready, and serve me while I eat and drink; later you can eat and drink'? Does he thank that servant because he did what was commanded? In the same way, when you have done all that you were commanded, you should say, 'We are unworthy servants; we've only done our duty.'"

DAY TWENTY-SIX

A Friend Dies

Now a man was sick, Lazarus from Bethany, the village of Mary and her sister Martha. Mary was the one who anointed the Lord with perfume and wiped his feet with her hair, and it was her brother Lazarus who was sick. So the sisters sent a message to him: "Lord, the one you love is sick."

When Jesus heard it, he said, "This sickness will not end in death but is for the glory of God, so that the Son of God may be glorified through it." Now Jesus loved Martha, her sister, and Lazarus. So when he heard that he was sick, he stayed two more days in the place where he was. Then after that, he said to the disciples, "Let's go to Judea again."

"Rabbi," the disciples told him, "just now the Jews tried to stone you, and you're going there again?"

"Aren't there twelve hours in a day?" Jesus answered. "If anyone walks during the day, he doesn't stumble, because he sees the light of this world. But if anyone walks during the night, he does stumble, because the light is not in him."

He said this, and then he told them, "Our friend Lazarus has fallen asleep, but I'm on my way to wake him up."

Then the disciples said to him, "Lord, if he has fallen asleep, he will get well."

Jesus, however, was speaking about his death, but they thought he was speaking about natural sleep. So Jesus then told them plainly, "Lazarus has died. I'm glad for you that I wasn't there so that you may believe. But let's go to him."

Then Thomas (called "Twin") said to his fellow disciples, "Let's go too so that we may die with him."

Lazarus Is Raised from the Dead

When Jesus arrived, he found that Lazarus had already been in the tomb four days. Bethany was near Jerusalem (less than two miles away). Many of the Jews had come to Martha and Mary to comfort them about their brother.

As soon as Martha heard that Jesus was coming, she went to meet him, but Mary remained seated in the house. Then Martha said to Jesus, "Lord, if you had been here, my brother wouldn't have died. Yet even now I know that whatever you ask from God, God will give you."

"Your brother will rise again," Jesus told her.

Martha said to him, "I know that he will rise again in the resurrection at the last day."

Jesus said to her, "I am the resurrection and the life. The one who believes in me, even if he dies, will live. Everyone who lives and believes in me will never die. Do you believe this?"

"Yes, Lord," she told him, "I believe you are the Messiah, the Son of God, who comes into the world."

Having said this, she went back and called her sister Mary, saying in private, "The Teacher is here and is calling for you."

As soon as Mary heard this, she got up quickly and went to him. Jesus had not yet come into the village but was still in the place where Martha had met him. The Jews who were with her in the house consoling her saw that Mary got up quickly and went out. They followed her, supposing that she was going to the tomb to cry there.

As soon as Mary came to where Jesus was and saw him, she fell at his feet and told him, "Lord, if you had been here, my brother wouldn't have died!"

When Jesus saw her crying, and the Jews who had come with her crying, he was deeply moved in his spirit and troubled. "Where have you put him?" he asked.

"Lord," they told him, "come and see."

Jesus wept.

So the Jews said, "See how he loved him!" But some of them said, "Couldn't he who opened the blind man's eyes also have kept this man from dying?"

Then Jesus, deeply moved again, came to the tomb. It was a cave, and a stone was lying against it. "Remove the stone," Jesus said.

Martha, the dead man's sister, told him, "Lord, there is already a stench because he has been dead four days."

Jesus said to her, "Didn't I tell you that if you believed you would see the glory of God?"

So they removed the stone. Then Jesus raised his eyes and said, "Father, I thank you that you heard me. I know that you always hear me, but because of the crowd standing here I said this, so that they may believe you sent me." After he said this, he shouted with a loud voice, "Lazarus, come out!" The dead man came out bound hand and foot with linen strips and with his face wrapped in a cloth. Jesus said to them, "Unwrap him and let him go."

The Plot to Kill Jesus

Therefore, many of the Jews who came to Mary and saw what he did believed in him. But some of them went to the Pharisees and told them what Jesus had done.

So the chief priests and the Pharisees convened the Sanhedrin and were saying, "What are we going to do since this man is doing many signs? If we let him go on like this, everyone will believe in him, and the Romans will come and take away both our place and our nation."

One of them, Caiaphas, who was high priest that year, said to them, "You know nothing at all! You're not considering that it is to your advantage that one man should die for the people rather than the whole nation perish." He did not say this on his own, but being high priest that year he prophesied that Jesus was going to die for the nation, and not for the nation only, but also to unite the scattered children of God. So from that day on they plotted to kill him.

Jesus therefore no longer walked openly among the Jews but departed from there to the countryside near the wilderness, to a town called Ephraim, and he stayed there with the disciples.

Jesus Heals Ten Lepers

While traveling to Jerusalem, he passed between Samaria and Galilee. As he entered a village, ten men with leprosy met him. They stood at a distance and raised their voices, saying, "Jesus, Master, have mercy on us!"

When he saw them, he told them, "Go and show yourselves to the priests." And while they were going, they were cleansed.

But one of them, seeing that he was healed, returned and, with a loud voice, gave glory to God. He fell facedown at his feet, thanking him. And he was a Samaritan.

Then Jesus said, "Were not ten cleansed? Where are the nine? Didn't any return to give glory to God except this foreigner?" And he told him, "Get up and go on your way. Your faith has saved you."

The Coming of the Kingdom

When he was asked by the Pharisees when the kingdom of God would come, he answered them, "The kingdom of God is not coming with something observable; no one will say, 'See here!' or 'There!' For you see, the kingdom of God is in your midst."

Then he told the disciples, "The days are coming when you will long to see one of the days of the Son of Man, but you won't see it. They will say to you, 'See there!' or 'See here!' Don't follow or run after them. For as the lightning flashes from horizon to horizon and lights up the sky, so the Son of Man will be in his day. But first it is necessary that he suffer many things and be rejected by this generation.

"Just as it was in the days of Noah, so it will be in the days of the Son of Man: People went on eating, drinking, marrying and being given in marriage until the day Noah boarded the ark, and the flood came and destroyed them all. It will be the same as it was in the days of Lot: People went on eating, drinking, buying, selling, planting, building. But on the day Lot left Sodom, fire and sulfur rained from heaven and destroyed them all. It will be like that on the day the Son of Man is revealed. On that day, a man on the housetop, whose belongings are in the house, must not come down to get them. Likewise the man who is in the field must not turn back. Remember Lot's wife! Whoever tries to make his life secure will lose it, and whoever loses his life will preserve it. I tell you, on that night two will be in one bed; one will be taken and the other will be left. Two women will be grinding grain together; one will be taken and the other left."

"Where, Lord?" they asked him.

He said to them, "Where the corpse is, there also the vultures will be gathered."

DAY
TWENTY-SEVEN

Two Parables on Prayer

Now he told them a parable on the need for them to pray always and not give up. "There was a judge in a certain town who didn't fear God or respect people. And a widow in that town kept coming to him, saying, 'Give me justice against my adversary.'

"For a while he was unwilling, but later he said to himself, 'Even though I don't fear God or respect people, yet because this widow keeps pestering me, I will give her justice, so that she doesn't wear me out by her persistent coming.'"

Then the Lord said, "Listen to what the unjust judge says. Will not God grant justice to his elect who cry out to him day and night? Will he delay helping them? I tell you that he will swiftly grant them justice. Nevertheless, when the Son of Man comes, will he find faith on earth?"

He also told this parable to some who trusted in themselves that they were righteous and looked down on everyone else: "Two men went up to the temple to pray, one a Pharisee and the other a tax collector. The Pharisee was standing and praying like this about himself: 'God, I thank you that I'm not like other people—greedy, unrighteous, adulterers, or even like this tax collector. I fast twice a week; I give a tenth of everything I get.'

"But the tax collector, standing far off, would not even raise his eyes to heaven but kept striking his chest and saying, 'God, have mercy on me, a sinner!' I tell you, this one went down to his house justified rather than the other, because everyone who exalts himself will be humbled, but the one who humbles himself will be exalted."

Debating the Pharisees on Divorce

When Jesus had finished saying these things, he departed from Galilee and went to the region of Judea across the Jordan. Large crowds followed him again, as was his custom he taught them and healed them there. Some Pharisees approached him to test him. They asked, "Is it lawful for a man to divorce his wife on any grounds?"

"Haven't you read," he replied, "that he who created them in the beginning made them male and female, and he also said, 'For this reason a man will leave his father and mother and be joined to his wife, and the two will become one flesh'? So they are no longer two, but one flesh. Therefore, what God has joined together, let no one separate."

"Why then," they asked him, "did Moses command us to give divorce papers and to send her away?"

He told them, "Moses permitted you to divorce your wives because of the hardness of your hearts, but it was not like that from the beginning. I tell you, whoever divorces his wife, except for sexual immorality, and marries another commits adultery. Also, if she divorces her husband and marries another, she commits adultery."

When they were in the house again, his disciples said to him, "If the relationship of a man with his wife is like this, it's better not to marry."

He responded, "Not everyone can accept this saying, but only those to whom it has been given. For there are eunuchs who were born that way from their mother's womb, there are eunuchs who were made by men, and there are eunuchs who have made themselves that way because of the kingdom of heaven. The one who is able to accept it should accept it."

Let the Children Come

Then people were bringing little children and infants to him in order that he might touch them and pray, but the disciples rebuked them. When Jesus saw it, he was indignant and said to them, "Let the little children come to me. Don't stop them, because the kingdom of God belongs to such as these. Truly I tell you, whoever does not receive the kingdom of God like a little child will never enter it." After taking them in his arms, he laid his hands on them and blessed them, then he went on from there.

The Rich Young Ruler

As he was setting out on a journey, a ruler ran up, knelt down before him, and asked him, "Good teacher, what good must I do to inherit eternal life?"

"Why do you call me good?" Jesus asked him. "No one is good except God alone. If you want to enter into life, keep the commandments."

"Which ones?" he asked him.

"You know the commandments: Do not murder; do not commit adultery; do not steal; do not bear false witness; do not defraud; honor your father and mother, and love your neighbor as yourself."

The young man told him, "Teacher, I have kept all these from my youth. What do I still lack?"

Looking at him, Jesus heard him and loved him. "You lack one thing if you want to be perfect: Go, sell all you have and give to the poor, and you will have treasure in heaven. Then come, follow me." But he was dismayed by this demand, and went away grieving and became extremely sad, because he was very rich and had many possessions.

Jesus looked around and said to his disciples, "How hard it is for those who have wealth to enter the kingdom of God!"

The disciples were astonished at his words. Again Jesus said to them, "Children, how hard it is to enter the kingdom of God! It is easier for a camel to go through the eye of a needle than for a rich person to enter the kingdom of God."

They were even more astonished, saying to one another, "Then who can be saved?"

Looking at them, Jesus said, "With man it is impossible, but not with God, because all things are possible with God."

The First Will Be Last, and the Last Will Be First

Peter began to tell him, "Look, we have left everything and followed you."

Jesus said to them, "Truly I tell you, in the renewal of all things, when the Son of Man sits on his glorious throne, you who have followed me will also sit on twelve thrones, judging the twelve tribes of Israel.

"Truly I tell you," Jesus said, "there is no one who has left house or wife or brothers or sisters or mother or father or children or fields for my sake and for the sake of the gospel, who will not receive a hundred times more, now at this time—houses, brothers and sisters, mothers and children, and fields, with persecutions—and eternal life in the age to come. But many who are first will be last, and the last first."

"For the kingdom of heaven is like a landowner who went out early in the morning to hire workers for his vineyard. After agreeing with the workers on one denarius, he sent them into his vineyard for the day. When he went out about nine in the morning, he saw others standing in the marketplace doing nothing. He said to them, 'You also go into my vineyard, and I'll give you whatever is right.' So off they went. About noon and about three, he went out again and did the same thing. Then about five he went and found others standing around and said to them, 'Why have you been standing here all day doing nothing?'

"'Because no one hired us,' they said to him.

"'You also go into my vineyard,' he told them. When evening came, the owner of the vineyard told his foreman, 'Call the workers and give them their pay, starting with the last and ending with the first.'

"When those who were hired about five came, they each received one denarius. So when the first ones came, they assumed they would get more, but they also received a denarius each. When they received it, they began to complain to the landowner: 'These last men put in one hour, and you made them equal to us who bore the burden of the day's work and the burning heat.'

"He replied to one of them, 'Friend, I'm doing you no wrong. Didn't you agree with me on a denarius? Take what's yours and go. I want to give this last man the same as I gave you. Don't I have the right to do what I want with what is mine? Are you jealous because I'm generous?'

"So the last will be first, and the first last."

DAY
TWENTY-EIGHT

A Lesson on Ambition

They were on the road, going up to Jerusalem, and Jesus was walking ahead of them. The disciples were astonished, but those who followed him were afraid. Taking the twelve disciples aside again, he began to tell them the things that would happen to him. "See, we are going up to Jerusalem. The Son of Man will be handed over to the chief priests and the scribes, and they will condemn him to death. Then they will hand him over to the Gentiles, and they will mock him, spit on him, flog him, and kill him, and he will rise after three days."

They understood none of these things. The meaning of the saying was hidden from them, and they did not grasp what was said.

Then the mother of James and John (Zebedee's sons), approached him with her sons. She knelt down. They said, "Teacher, we want you to do whatever we ask you."

"What do you want me to do for you?" he asked them.

"Promise," she said to him, "that these two sons of mine may sit, one on your right and the other on your left, in your kingdom."

Jesus answered, "You don't know what you're asking. Are you able to drink the cup that I am about to drink or to be baptized with the baptism I am baptized with?"

"We are able," they told him.

Jesus said to them, "You will drink the cup I drink, and you will be baptized with the baptism I am baptized with. But to sit at my right or left is not mine to give; instead, it is for those for whom it has been prepared."

When the ten disciples heard this, they began to be indignant with James and John. Jesus called them over and said to them, "You know that those who are regarded as rulers of the Gentiles lord it over them, and those in high positions act as tyrants over them. But it is not so among you. On the contrary, whoever wants to become great among you will be your servant, and whoever wants to be first among you will be a slave to all. For even the Son of Man did not come to be served, but to serve, and to give his life as a ransom for many."

Blind Bartimaeus

They came to Jericho. And as he approached Jericho with his disciples and a large crowd, Bartimaeus (the son of Timaeus), a blind beggar, was sitting by the road. Hearing a crowd passing by, he inquired what was happening. "Jesus of Nazareth is passing by," they told him.

So he called out, "Jesus, Son of David, have mercy on me!" Then those in front told him to keep quiet, but he kept crying out all the more, "Son of David, have mercy on me!"

Jesus stopped and said, "Call him."

So they called the blind man and said to him, "Have courage! Get up; he's calling for you." He threw off his coat, jumped up, and came to Jesus.

Then Jesus answered him, "What do you want me to do for you?"

"*Rabboni*," the blind man said to him, "I want to see."

Moved with compassion, Jesus said to him, "Go, your faith has saved you." Jesus touched his eyes. Instantly he could see, and he began to follow Jesus on the road, glorifying God. All the people, when they saw it, gave praise to God.

Zacchaeus Wanted to See

He entered Jericho and was passing through. There was a man named Zacchaeus who was a chief tax collector, and he was rich. He was trying to see who Jesus was, but he was not able because of the crowd, since he was a short man. So running ahead, he climbed up a syca-more tree to see Jesus, since he was about to pass that way. When Jesus came to the place, he looked up and said to him, "Zacchaeus, hurry and come down because today it is necessary for me to stay at your house."

So he quickly came down and welcomed him joyfully. All who saw it began to complain, "He's gone to stay with a sinful man."

But Zacchaeus stood there and said to the Lord, "Look, I'll give half of my possessions to the poor, Lord. And if I have extorted anything from anyone, I'll pay back four times as much."

"Today salvation has come to this house," Jesus told him, "because he too is a son of Abraham. For the Son of Man has come to seek and to save the lost."

Parable of the Ten Minas

As they were listening to this, he went on to tell a parable because he was near Jerusalem, and they thought the kingdom of God was going to appear right away.

Therefore he said, "A nobleman traveled to a far country to receive for himself authority to be king and then to return. He called ten of his servants, gave them ten minas,[1] and told them, 'Engage in business until I come back.'

"But his subjects hated him and sent a delegation after him, saying, 'We don't want this man to rule over us.'

"At his return, having received the authority to be king, he summoned those servants he had given the money to, so that he could find out how much they

---

1   A mina was worth about a hundred days' wages.

had made in business. The first came forward and said, 'Master, your mina has earned ten more minas.'

"'Well done, good servant!' he told him. 'Because you have been faithful in a very small matter, have authority over ten towns.'

"The second came and said, 'Master, your mina has made five minas.'

"So he said to him, 'You will be over five towns.'

"And another came and said, 'Master, here is your mina. I have kept it safe in a cloth because I was afraid of you since you're a harsh man: you collect what you didn't deposit and reap what you didn't sow.'

"He told him, 'I will condemn you by what you have said, you evil servant! If you knew I was a harsh man, collecting what I didn't deposit and reaping what I didn't sow, why, then, didn't you put my money in the bank? And when I returned, I would have collected it with interest.' So he said to those standing there, 'Take the mina away from him and give it to the one who has ten minas.'

"But they said to him, 'Master, he has ten minas.'

"'I tell you, that to everyone who has, more will be given; and from the one who does not have, even what he does have will be taken away. But bring here these enemies of mine, who did not want me to rule over them, and slaughter them in my presence.'"

Mary Anoints Jesus for Burial

Now the Jewish Passover was near, and many went up to Jerusalem from the country to purify themselves before the Passover. They were looking for Jesus and asking one another as they stood in the temple, "What do you think? He won't come to the festival, will he?" The chief priests and the Pharisees had given orders that if anyone knew where he was, he should report it so that they could arrest him.

Six days before the Passover, Jesus came to Bethany at the house of Simon the leper where Lazarus was, the one Jesus had raised from the dead. So they gave a dinner for him there; Martha was serving them, and Lazarus was one of those reclining at the table with him. Then Mary took an alabaster jar of a pound of perfume, pure and expensive nard. She broke the jar and poured it on his head. Then she anointed Jesus's feet and wiped his feet with her hair. So the house was filled with the fragrance of the perfume.

But some disciples were expressing indignation to one another: "Why has this perfume been wasted?" And they began to scold her. Then one of his disciples, Judas Iscariot (who was about to betray him), said, "Why wasn't this perfume sold for three hundred denarii and given to the poor?" He didn't say this because he cared about the poor but because he was a thief. He was in charge of the money-bag and would steal part of what was put in it.

Jesus replied, "Leave her alone. Why are you bothering her? She has done a noble thing for me. She has kept it for the day of my burial. For you always have the poor with you, but you do not always have me. By pouring this perfume on my body she has anointed me in advance for burial. Truly I tell you, wherever the gospel is proclaimed in the whole world, what she has done will also be told in memory of her."

Then a large crowd of the Jews learned he was there. They came not only because of Jesus but also to see Lazarus, the one he had raised from the dead. But the chief priests had decided to kill Lazarus also, because he was the reason many of the Jews were deserting them and believing in Jesus.

DAY
TWENTY-NINE

The Triumphal Entry

When they approached Jerusalem, at Bethphage and Bethany near the Mount of Olives, he sent two of his disciples and told them, "Go into the village ahead of you. As soon as you enter it, you will find a donkey tied there with her colt, on which no one has ever sat. Untie them and bring them. If anyone says to you, 'Why are you doing this?' say, 'The Lord needs it and will send it back here right away.'"

So those who were sent left and found it just as he had told them. As they were untying the colt, its owners said to them, "Why are you untying the colt?" They answered them just as Jesus had said; so they let them go.

They brought the donkey and the colt to Jesus and threw their clothes on them, and he sat on the colt.

This took place so that what was spoken through the prophet might be fulfilled:

Tell Daughter Zion,
"See, your King is coming to you,
gentle, and mounted on a donkey,
and on a colt,
the foal of a donkey."

As he was going along, many people spread their clothes on the road, and others spread palm branches cut from the trees in the fields. Now he came near the path down the Mount of Olives, and the whole crowd of the disciples began to praise God joyfully with a loud voice for all the miracles they had seen.

Then the crowds who went ahead of him and those who followed shouted:

Hosanna to the Son of David!
Blessed is he who comes in the name
of the Lord!
Hosanna in the highest heaven!

His disciples did not understand these things at first. However, when Jesus was glorified, then they remembered that these things had been written about him and that they had done these things to him.

Meanwhile, the crowd, which had been with him when he called Lazarus out of the tomb and raised him from the dead, continued to testify. This is also why the crowd met him, because they heard he had done this sign.

Some of the Pharisees from the crowd told him, "Teacher, rebuke your disciples."

He answered, "I tell you, if they were to keep silent, the stones would cry out."

Then the Pharisees said to one another, "You see? You've accomplished nothing. Look, the world has gone after him!"

As he approached and saw the city, he wept for it, saying, "If you knew this day what would bring peace—but now it is hidden from your eyes. For the days will come on you when your enemies will build a barricade around you, surround you, and hem you in on every side. They will crush you and your children among you to the ground, and they will not leave one stone on another in your midst, because you did not recognize the time when God visited you."

When he entered Jerusalem, the whole city was in an uproar, saying, "Who is this?" The crowds were saying, "This is the prophet Jesus from Nazareth in Galilee."

The blind and the lame came to him in the temple, and he healed them. When the chief priests and the scribes saw the wonders that he did and the children shouting in the temple, "*Hosanna* to the Son of David!" they were indignant and said to him, "Do you hear what these children are saying?"

Jesus replied, "Yes, have you never read:

You have prepared praise
from the mouths of infants and nursing
babies?"

Jesus went into Jerusalem and into the temple. After looking around at everything, since it was already late, he went out of the city to Bethany with the Twelve and spent the night there.

Cursing of the Fig Tree

The next day, early in the morning, when they went out from Bethany, on his way back to the city, Jesus was hungry. Seeing in the distance by the road a fig tree with leaves, he went to find out if there was anything on it. When he came to it, he found nothing but leaves; for it was not the season for figs. He said to it, "May no one ever eat fruit from you again!" And his disciples heard it. At once the fig tree withered.

Jesus Cleanses the Temple

They came to Jerusalem, and he went into the temple and began to throw out all those buying and selling. He overturned the tables of the money changers and the chairs of those selling doves, and would not permit anyone to carry goods through the temple. He was teaching them: "Is it not written, 'My house will be called a house of prayer for all nations?' But you have made it 'a den of thieves!'"

The chief priests and the scribes heard it and started looking for a way to kill him. For they were afraid of him, because the whole crowd was astonished by his teaching and were captivated by what they heard.

Greeks Want to See Jesus

Now some Greeks were among those who went up to worship at the festival. So they came to Philip, who was from Bethsaida in Galilee, and requested of him, "Sir, we want to see Jesus." Philip went and told Andrew; then Andrew and Philip went and told Jesus.

Jesus replied to them, "The hour has come for the Son of Man to be glorified. Truly I tell you, unless a grain of wheat falls to the ground and dies, it remains by itself. But if it dies, it produces much fruit. The one who loves his life will lose it, and the one who hates his life in this world will keep it for eternal life. If anyone serves me, he must follow me. Where I am, there my servant also will be. If anyone serves me, the Father will honor him.

"Now my soul is troubled. What should I say—Father, save me from this hour? But that is why I came to this hour. Father, glorify your name."

Then a voice came from heaven: "I have glorified it, and I will glorify it again."

The crowd standing there heard it and said it was thunder. Others said, "An angel has spoken to him."

Jesus responded, "This voice came, not for me, but for you. Now is the judgment of this world. Now the ruler of this world will be cast out. As for me, if I am lifted up from the earth I will draw all people to myself." He said this to indicate what kind of death he was about to die.

Then the crowd replied to him, "We have heard from the law that the Messiah will remain forever. So how can you say, 'The Son of Man must be lifted up'? Who is this Son of Man?"

Jesus answered, "The light will be with you only a little longer. Walk while you have the light so that darkness doesn't overtake you. The one who walks in darkness doesn't know where he's going. While you have the light, believe in the light so that you may become children of light." Jesus said this, then went away and hid from them.

Isaiah's Prophecies Fulfilled

Even though he had performed so many signs in their presence, they did not believe in him. This was to fulfill the word of Isaiah the prophet, who said:

> Lord, who has believed our message?
> And to whom has the arm of the Lord been revealed?

This is why they were unable to believe, because Isaiah also said:

> He has blinded their eyes
> and hardened their hearts,
> so that they would not see with their eyes
> or understand with their hearts,
> and turn,
> and I would heal them.

Isaiah said these things because he saw his glory and spoke about him.

Nevertheless, many did believe in him even among the rulers, but because of the Pharisees they did not confess him, so that they would not be banned from the synagogue. For they loved human praise more than praise from God.

Jesus cried out, "The one who believes in me believes not in me, but in him who sent me. And the one who sees me sees him who sent me. I have come as light into the world, so that everyone who believes in me would not remain in darkness. If anyone hears my words and doesn't keep them, I do not judge him; for I did not come to judge the world but to save the world. The one who rejects me and doesn't receive my sayings has this as his judge: The word I have spoken will judge him on the last day. For I have not spoken on my own, but the Father himself who sent me has given me a command to say everything I have said. I know that his command is eternal life. So the things that I speak, I speak just as the Father has told me."

DAY THIRTY

Lessons from the Withered Fig Tree

Early in the morning, as they were passing by, they saw the fig tree withered from the roots up. Then Peter remembered and said to him, "Rabbi, look! The fig tree that you cursed has withered."

Jesus replied to them, "Have faith in God.

"Truly I tell you, if you have faith and do not doubt, you will not only do what was done to the fig tree, but even if you tell this mountain, 'Be lifted up and thrown into the sea,' it will be done. Therefore I tell you, everything you pray and ask for—believe that you have received it and it will be yours. And whenever you stand praying, if you have anything against anyone, forgive him, so that your Father in heaven will also forgive you your wrongdoing."

During the day, he was teaching in the temple, but in the evening he would go out and spend the night on what is called the Mount of Olives. Then all the people would come early in the morning to hear him in the temple.

Jesus' Authority Challenged by the Sanhedrin

They came again to Jerusalem. As he was walking in the temple, teaching the people and proclaiming the good news, the chief priests, the scribes, and the elders came and asked him, "Tell us, by what authority are you doing these things? Who gave you this authority to do these things?"

Jesus said to them, "I will also ask you one question; then answer me, and I will tell you by what authority I do these things. Was John's baptism from heaven or of human origin? Answer me."

They discussed it among themselves: "If we say, 'From heaven,' he will say, 'Then why didn't you believe him?' But if we say, 'Of human origin'—all the people will stone us, because they are convinced that John was truly a prophet." So they answered Jesus, "We don't know."

And Jesus said to them, "Neither will I tell you by what authority I do these things."

Parable of the Two Sons

"What do you think? A man had two sons. He went to the first and said, 'My son, go work in the vineyard today.'

"He answered, 'I don't want to,' but later he changed his mind and went. Then the man went to the other and said the same thing. 'I will, sir,' he answered, but he didn't go. Which of the two did his father's will?"

They said, "The first."

Jesus said to them, "Truly I tell you, tax collectors and prostitutes are entering the kingdom of God before you. For John came to you in the way of righteousness, and you didn't believe him. Tax collectors and prostitutes did believe him; but you, when you saw it, didn't even change your minds then and believe him.

Parable of the Vineyard

"Listen to another parable: There was a landowner, who planted a vineyard, put a fence around it, dug a winepress in it, and built a watchtower. He leased it to tenant farmers and went away for a long time. When the time came to harvest fruit, he sent a servant to the farmers to collect some of his fruit of the vineyard. The farmers took him, beat him, and sent him away empty-handed. He sent another servant to them, and they hit him on the head and treated him shamefully. And he sent yet a third, but they wounded this one too and threw him out. Then he sent another, and they killed that one. He also sent many others; some they beat, and others they killed.

"He still had one to send. The owner of the vineyard said, 'What should I do? I will send my beloved son. Perhaps they will respect him.'

"But when the tenant farmers saw the son, they discussed it among themselves, 'This is the heir. Come, let's kill him and take his inheritance.' So they seized him, threw him out of the vineyard, and killed him.

"Therefore, when the owner of the vineyard comes, what will he do to those farmers?"

"He will completely destroy those terrible men," they told him, "and lease his vineyard to other farmers who will give him his fruit at the harvest."

Jesus said to them, "Have you never read in the Scriptures:

> The stone that the builders rejected
> has become the cornerstone.
> This is what the Lord has done
> and it is wonderful in our eyes?

"Therefore I tell you, the kingdom of God will be taken away from you and given to a people producing its fruit. Whoever falls on this stone will be broken to pieces; but on whomever it falls, it will shatter him."

The Pharisees and the chief priests looked for a way to get their hands on him and arrest him that very hour, because they knew he had told this parable against them, but they feared the crowds because the people regarded him as a prophet. So they left him and went away.

Parable of the Wedding Banquet

Once more Jesus spoke to them in parables: "The kingdom of heaven is like a king who gave a wedding banquet for his son. He sent his servants to summon those invited to the banquet, but they didn't want to come. Again, he sent out other servants and said, 'Tell those who are invited: See, I've prepared my dinner; my oxen and fattened cattle have been slaughtered, and everything is ready. Come to the wedding banquet.'

"But they paid no attention and went away, one to his own farm, another to his business, while the rest seized his servants, mistreated them, and killed them. The king was enraged, and he sent out his troops, killed those murderers, and burned down their city.

"Then he told his servants, 'The banquet is ready, but those who were invited were not worthy. Go then to where the roads exit the city and invite everyone you find to the banquet.' So those servants went out on the roads and gathered everyone they found, both evil and good. The wedding banquet was filled with guests. When the king came in to see the guests, he saw a man there who was not dressed for a wedding. So he said to him, 'Friend, how did you get in here without wedding clothes?' The man was speechless.

"Then the king told the attendants, 'Tie him up hand and foot, and throw him into the outer darkness, where there will be weeping and gnashing of teeth.'

"For many are invited, but few are chosen."

A Question about Taxes

Then the Pharisees went and plotted how to trap him by what he said to hand him over to the governor's rule and authority. So they sent their disciples to him, along with the Herodians, spies who pretended to be righteous. "Teacher," they said, "we know that you are truthful and teach truthfully the way of God. You don't care what anyone thinks nor do you show partiality. Tell us, then, what you think. Is it lawful to pay taxes to Caesar or not? Should we pay or shouldn't we?"

Perceiving their malicious intent, Jesus said, "Why are you testing me, hypocrites? Show me the coin used for the tax." They brought him a denarius. "Whose image and inscription is this?" he asked them.

"Caesar's," they said to him.

Then he said to them, "Give, then, to Caesar the things that are Caesar's, and to God the things that are God's." They were not able to catch him in what he said in public, and being utterly amazed at his answer, they became silent. So they left him and went away.

A Question about the Resurrection

That same day some Sadducees, who say there is no resurrection, came to him and questioned him: "Teacher, Moses wrote for us that if a man's brother dies, leaving a wife behind but no child, that man should take the wife and raise up offspring for his brother. There were seven brothers among us. The first married a woman, and dying, left no offspring. The second also took her, and he died, leaving no offspring. And the third likewise. None of the seven left offspring. Last of all, the woman died too. In the resurrection, when they rise, whose wife will she be, since the seven had married her?"

Jesus spoke to them, "Isn't this the reason why you're mistaken: you don't know the Scriptures or the power of God? The children of this age marry and are given in marriage. But those who are counted worthy to take part in that age and in the resurrection from the dead neither marry nor are given in marriage. For they can no longer die, because they are like angels in heaven and are children of God, since they are children of the resurrection.

"And as for the dead being raised—haven't you read in the book of Moses? Moses even indicated in the passage about the burning bush that the dead are raised, where he calls the Lord the God of Abraham and the God of Isaac and the God of Jacob. He is not the God of the dead but of the living, because all are living to him. You are badly mistaken."

And when the crowds heard this, they were astonished at his teaching.

Some of the scribes answered, "Teacher, you have spoken well." And they no longer dared to ask him anything.

DAY
THIRTY-ONE

The Greatest Commandment

When the Pharisees heard that he had silenced the Sadducees, they came together. One of the scribes, an expert in the law, approached. When he heard them debating and saw that Jesus answered them well, he asked a question to test him, "Which command is the most important of all?"

Jesus answered, "The most important is *Listen, Israel! The Lord our God, the Lord is one. Love the Lord your God with all your heart, with all your soul, with all your mind, and with all your strength.* This is the greatest and most important command. The second is like it: *Love your neighbor as yourself.* There is no other command greater than these. All the Law and the Prophets depend on these two commands."

While the Pharisees were together, Jesus was teaching in the temple and questioned them, "What do you think about the Messiah? Whose son is he?"

They replied, "David's."

He asked them, "How can the scribes say that the Messiah is the son of David? How is it then that David, inspired by the Holy Spirit, calls him 'Lord'? For David himself says in the Book of Psalms:

> The Lord declared to my Lord,
> 'Sit at my right hand
> until I put your enemies under your feet'?

"If David calls him 'Lord,' how, then, can he be his son?" No one was able to answer him at all, and from that day no one dared to question him anymore. And the large crowd was listening to him with delight.

Religious Hypocrites Denounced

Then Jesus spoke to the crowds and to his disciples: "The scribes and the Pharisees are seated in the chair of Moses. Therefore do whatever they tell you, and observe it. But don't do what they do, because they don't practice what they teach. They tie up heavy loads that are hard to carry and put them on people's shoulders, but they themselves aren't willing to lift a finger to move them. They do everything to be seen by others: They enlarge their phylacteries and lengthen their tassels. They love the place of honor at banquets, the front seats in the synagogues, greetings in the marketplaces, and to be called 'Rabbi' by people.

"But you are not to be called 'Rabbi,' because you have one Teacher, and you are all brothers and sisters. Do not call anyone on earth your father, because you have one Father, who is in heaven. You are not to be called instructors either, because you have one

Instructor, the Messiah. The greatest among you will be your servant. Whoever exalts himself will be humbled, and whoever humbles himself will be exalted.

"Woe to you, scribes and Pharisees, hypocrites! You shut the door of the kingdom of heaven in people's faces. For you don't go in, and you don't allow those entering to go in.

"They devour widows' houses and say long prayers just for show. These will receive harsher judgment.

"Woe to you, scribes and Pharisees, hypocrites! You travel over land and sea to make one convert, and when he becomes one, you make him twice as much a child of hell as you are!

"Woe to you, blind guides, who say, 'Whoever takes an oath by the temple, it means nothing. But whoever takes an oath by the gold of the temple is bound by his oath.' Blind fools! For which is greater, the gold or the temple that sanctified the gold? Also, 'Whoever takes an oath by the altar, it means nothing; but whoever takes an oath by the gift that is on it is bound by his oath.' Blind people! For which is greater, the gift or the altar that sanctifies the gift? Therefore, the one who takes an oath by the altar takes an oath by it and by everything on it. The one who takes an oath by the temple takes an oath by it and by him who dwells in it. And the one who takes an oath by heaven takes an oath by God's throne and by him who sits on it.

"Woe to you, scribes and Pharisees, hypocrites! You pay a tenth of mint, dill, and cumin, and yet you have neglected the more important matters of the law—justice, mercy, and faithfulness. These things should have been done without neglecting the others. Blind guides! You strain out a gnat, but gulp down a camel!

"Woe to you, scribes and Pharisees, hypocrites! You clean the outside of the cup and dish, but inside they are full of greed and self-indulgence. Blind Pharisee! First clean the inside of the cup, so that the outside of it may also become clean.

"Woe to you, scribes and Pharisees, hypocrites! You are like whitewashed tombs, which appear beautiful on the outside, but inside are full of the bones of the dead and every kind of impurity. In the same way, on the outside you seem righteous to people, but inside you are full of hypocrisy and lawlessness.

"Woe to you, scribes and Pharisees, hypocrites! You build the tombs of the prophets and decorate the graves of the righteous, and you say, 'If we had lived in the days of our ancestors, we wouldn't have taken part with them in shedding the prophets' blood.' So you testify against yourselves that you are descendants of those who murdered the prophets. Fill up, then, the measure of your ancestors' sins!

"Snakes! Brood of vipers! How can you escape being condemned to hell? This is why I am sending you prophets, sages, and scribes. Some of them you will kill and crucify, and some of them you will flog in your synagogues and pursue from town to town. So all the righteous blood shed on the earth will be charged to you, from the blood of righteous Abel to the blood of Zechariah, son of Berechiah, whom you murdered between the sanctuary and the altar. Truly I tell you, all these things will come on this generation.

"Jerusalem, Jerusalem, who kills the prophets and stones those who are sent to her. How often I wanted to gather your children together, as a hen gathers her chicks under her wings, but you were not willing! See, your house is left to you desolate. For I tell you, you will not see me again until you say, 'Blessed is he who comes in the name of the Lord'!"

A Widow's Gift

Sitting across from the temple treasury, he watched how the crowd dropped money into the treasury. He looked up and saw many rich people were putting in large sums. Then a poor widow came and dropped in two tiny coins worth very little. Summoning his disciples, he said to them, "Truly I tell you, this poor widow has put more into the treasury than all the others. For they all gave out of their surplus, but she out of her poverty has put in everything she had—all she had to live on."

Signs of the End of the Age

As Jesus left and was going out of the temple, his disciples came up and called his attention to its buildings. "Teacher, look! What massive stones! What impressive buildings! Adorned with beautiful stones and gifts dedicated to God."

He replied to them, "Do you see all these things? Truly I tell you, the days will come when not one stone will be left here on another that will not be thrown down."

While he was sitting on the Mount of Olives across from the temple, Peter, James, John, and Andrew approached him privately and said, "Tell us, when will these things happen? And what is the sign of your coming and of the end of the age?"

Jesus replied to them, "Watch out that no one deceives you. For many will come in my name, saying, 'I am the Messiah,' and, 'The time is near,' and they will deceive many. Don't follow them. You are going to hear of wars and rumors of wars. See that you are not alarmed, because these things must take place first, but the end is not yet. For nation will rise up against nation, and kingdom against kingdom. There will be earthquakes and famines and plagues and there will be terrifying sights and great signs from heaven in various places. All these events are the beginning of labor pains.

"But you, be on your guard! Before all these things, they will lay their hands on you and persecute you and they will kill you. They will hand you over to local courts, and you will be flogged in the synagogues and prisons, and you will be brought before kings and governors because of my name. This will give you an opportunity to bear witness. Therefore make up your minds not to prepare your defense ahead of time, for I will give you such words and a wisdom that none of your adversaries will be able to resist or contradict, for it isn't you speaking, but the Holy Spirit. You will even be betrayed by parents, brothers, relatives, and friends. They will kill some of you. You will be hated by everyone because of my name, but not a hair of your head will be lost.

"Then many will fall away, betray one another, and hate one another. Many false prophets will rise up and deceive many. Because lawlessness will multiply, the love of many will grow cold. But the one who endures to the end will be saved; by your endurance, gain your lives. This good news of the kingdom will be proclaimed in all the world as a testimony to all nations, and then the end will come."

DAY THIRTY-TWO

The Abomination of Desolation

"So when you see the abomination of desolation, spoken of by the prophet Daniel, standing in the holy place where it should not be, when you see Jerusalem surrounded by armies, then those in Judea must flee to the mountains (let the reader understand). A man on the housetop must not come down to get things out of his house, and a man in the field must not go back to get his coat. Those inside the city must leave it, and those who are in the country must not enter it, because these are days of vengeance to fulfill all the things that are written. There will be great distress in the land and wrath against this people. They will be killed by the sword and be led captive into all the nations, and Jerusalem will be trampled by the Gentiles until the times of the Gentiles are fulfilled.

"Woe to pregnant women and nursing mothers in those days! Pray that your escape may not be in winter or on a Sabbath. For at that time there will be great distress, the kind that hasn't taken place from the beginning of creation until now and never will again. Unless those days were cut short, no one would be saved. But those days will be cut short because of the elect whom he chose.

"If anyone tells you then, 'See, here is the Messiah!' or, 'Over here!' do not believe it. For false messiahs and false prophets will arise and perform great signs and wonders to lead astray, if possible, even the elect. And you must watch! Take note: I have told you in advance. So if they tell you, 'See, he's in the wilderness!' don't go out; or, 'See, he's in the storerooms!' do not believe it. For as the lightning comes from the east and flashes as far as the west, so will be the coming of the Son of Man. Wherever the carcass is, there the vultures will gather.

The Coming of the Son of Man

"Immediately after the distress of those days there will be signs in the sun, moon, and stars. The sun will be darkened, and the moon will not shed its light; the stars will fall from the sky. There will be anguish on the earth among nations bewildered by the roaring of the sea and the waves. People will faint from fear and expectation of the things that are coming on the world, because the powers of the heavens will be shaken. Then the sign of the Son of Man will appear in the sky, and then all the peoples of the earth will mourn; and they will see the Son of Man coming on the clouds of heaven with power and great glory. He will send out his angels with a loud trumpet, and they will gather his elect from the four winds, from one end of the sky to the other."

The Time Is Near

"When these things begin to take place, stand up and lift your heads, because your redemption is near.

"Learn this lesson from the fig tree: As soon as its branch becomes tender and sprouts leaves, you know that summer is near. In the same way, when you see all these things happening, recognize that he is near—at the door.

"Truly I tell you, this generation will certainly not pass away until all these things take place. Heaven and earth will pass away, but my words will never pass away.

"Now concerning that day and hour no one knows—neither the angels of heaven nor the Son— except the Father alone. As the days of Noah were, so the coming of the Son of Man will be. For in those days before the flood they were eating and drinking, marrying and giving in marriage, until the day Noah boarded the ark. They didn't know until the flood came and swept them all away. This is the way the coming of the Son of Man will be. Then two men will be in the field; one will be taken and one left. Two women will be grinding grain with a hand mill; one will be taken and one left.

"Watch! Be alert! For you don't know when the time is coming."

Stay Alert and Be Ready

"Be on your guard, so that your minds are not dulled from carousing, drunkenness, and worries of life, or that day will come on you unexpectedly like a trap. For it will come on all who live on the face of the whole earth. But be alert at all times, praying that you may have strength to escape all these things that are going to take place and to stand before the Son of Man.

"It is like a man on a journey, who left his house, gave authority to his servants, gave each one his work, and commanded the doorkeeper to be alert. But know this: If the homeowner had known what time the thief was coming, he would have stayed alert and not let his house be broken into. This is why you are also to be ready, because the Son of Man is coming at an hour you do not expect.

"Who then is a faithful and wise servant, whom his master has put in charge of his household, to give them food at the proper time? Blessed is that servant whom the master finds doing his job when he comes. Truly I tell you, he will put him in charge of all his possessions. But if that wicked servant says in his heart, 'My master is delayed,' and starts to beat his fellow servants, and eats and drinks with drunkards, that servant's master will come on a day he does not expect him and at an hour he does not know. He will cut him to pieces and assign him a place with the hypocrites, where there will be weeping and gnashing of teeth.

"At that time the kingdom of heaven will be like ten virgins who took their lamps and went out to meet the groom. Five of them were foolish and five were wise. When the foolish took their lamps, they didn't take oil with them; but the wise ones took oil in their flasks with their lamps. When the groom was delayed, they all became drowsy and fell asleep.

"In the middle of the night there was a shout: 'Here's the groom! Come out to meet him.'

"Then all the virgins got up and trimmed their lamps. The foolish ones said to the wise ones, 'Give us some of your oil, because our lamps are going out.'

"The wise ones answered, 'No, there won't be enough for us and for you. Go instead to those who sell oil, and buy some for yourselves.'

"When they had gone to buy some, the groom arrived, and those who were ready went in with him to the wedding banquet, and the door was shut. Later the rest of the virgins also came and said, 'Master, master, open up for us!'

"He replied, 'Truly I tell you, I don't know you!'

"Therefore be alert, because you don't know either the day or the hour.

"For it is just like a man about to go on a journey. He called his own servants and entrusted his possessions to them. To one he gave five talents, to another two talents, and to another one talent, depending on each one's ability. Then he went on a journey. Immediately the man who had received five talents went, put them to work, and earned five more. In the same way the man with two earned two more. But the man who had received one talent went off, dug a hole in the ground, and hid his master's money.

"After a long time the master of those servants came and settled accounts with them. The man who had received five talents approached, presented five more talents, and said, 'Master, you gave me five talents. See, I've earned five more talents.'

"His master said to him, 'Well done, good and faithful servant! You were faithful over a few things; I will put you in charge of many things. Share your master's joy.'

"The man with two talents also approached. He said, 'Master, you gave me two talents. See, I've earned two more talents.'

"His master said to him, 'Well done, good and faithful servant! You were faithful over a few things; I will put you in charge of many things. Share your master's joy.'

"The man who had received one talent also approached and said, 'Master, I know you. You're a harsh man, reaping where you haven't sown and gathering where you haven't scattered seed. So I was afraid and went off and hid your talent in the ground. See, you have what is yours.'

"His master replied to him, 'You evil, lazy servant! If you knew that I reap where I haven't sown and gather where I haven't scattered, then you should have deposited my money with the bankers, and I would have received my money back with interest when I returned.

"'So take the talent from him and give it to the one who has ten talents. For to everyone who has, more will be given, and he will have more than enough. But from the one who does not have, even what he has will be taken away from him. And throw this good-for-nothing servant into the outer darkness, where there will be weeping and gnashing of teeth.'

Therefore be alert, since you don't know what day your Lord is coming.

DAY
THIRTY-THREE

Judgment When the Son of Man Comes

"When the Son of Man comes in his glory, and all the angels with him, then he will sit on his glorious throne. All the nations will be gathered before him, and he will separate them one from another, just as a shepherd separates the sheep from the goats. He will put the sheep on his right and the goats on the left. Then the King will say to those on his right, 'Come, you who are blessed by my Father; inherit the kingdom prepared for you from the foundation of the world.

"'For I was hungry and you gave me something to eat; I was thirsty and you gave me something to drink; I was a stranger and you took me in; I was naked and you clothed me; I was sick and you took care of me; I was in prison and you visited me.'

"Then the righteous will answer him, 'Lord, when did we see you hungry and feed you, or thirsty and give you something to drink? When did we see you a stranger and take you in, or without clothes and clothe you? When did we see you sick, or in prison, and visit you?'

"And the King will answer them, 'Truly I tell you, whatever you did for one of the least of these brothers and sisters of mine, you did for me.'

"Then he will also say to those on the left, 'Depart from me, you who are cursed, into the eternal fire prepared for the devil and his angels! For I was hungry and you gave me nothing to eat; I was thirsty and you gave me nothing to drink; I was a stranger and you didn't take me in; I was naked and you didn't clothe me, sick and in prison and you didn't take care of me.'

"Then they too will answer, 'Lord, when did we see you hungry, or thirsty, or a stranger, or without clothes, or sick, or in prison, and not help you?'

"Then he will answer them, 'Truly I tell you, whatever you did not do for one of the least of these, you did not do for me.'

"And they will go away into eternal punishment, but the righteous into eternal life."

Betrayal Begins

When Jesus had finished saying all these things, he told his disciples, "You know that the Passover takes place after two days, and the Son of Man will be handed over to be crucified."

Then the chief priests and the elders of the people assembled in the courtyard of the high priest, who was named Caiaphas, and they conspired to arrest Jesus in a treacherous way and kill him. "Not during the festival," they said, "so there won't be rioting among the people."

Then Satan entered Judas, called Iscariot, who was numbered among the Twelve. He went away and discussed with the chief priests and temple police how he could hand him over to them. He said, "What are you willing to give me if I hand him over to you?" When they heard this, they were glad and agreed to give him silver. So they weighed out thirty pieces of silver for him. And from that time he started looking for a good opportunity to betray him to them when the crowd was not present.

Passover Preparation

On the first day of Unleavened Bread, when they sacrifice the Passover lamb, his disciples asked him, "Where do you want us to go and prepare the Passover so that you may eat it?"

So he sent two of his disciples, Peter and John, and told them, "Go into the city, and a man carrying a jar of water will meet you. Follow him. Wherever he enters, tell the owner of the house, 'The Teacher says, "My time is near. Where is my guest room where I may eat the Passover with my disciples?"' He will show you a large room upstairs, furnished and ready. Make the preparations for us there." So the disciples went out, entered the city, and found it just as he had told them, and they prepared the Passover.

When the hour came, he reclined at the table, and the apostles with him. Then he said to them, "I have fervently desired to eat this Passover with you before I suffer. For I tell you, I will not eat it again until it is fulfilled in the kingdom of God."

The Dispute over Greatness

Then a dispute also arose among them about who should be considered the greatest. But he said to them, "The kings of the Gentiles lord it over them, and those who have authority over them have themselves called 'Benefactors.' It is not to be like that among you. On the contrary, whoever is greatest among you should become like the youngest, and whoever leads, like the one serving. For who is greater, the one at the table or the one serving? Isn't it the one at the table? But I am among you as the one who serves. You are those who stood by me in my trials. I bestow on you a kingdom, just as my Father bestowed one on me, so that you may eat and drink at my table in my kingdom. And you will sit on thrones judging the twelve tribes of Israel."

Jesus Washes the Disciples' Feet

Before the Passover Festival, Jesus knew that his hour had come to depart from this world to the Father. Having loved his own who were in the world, he loved them to the end.

Now when it was time for supper, the devil had already put it into the heart of Judas, Simon Iscariot's son, to betray him. Jesus knew that the Father had given everything into his hands, that he had come from God, and that he was going back to God. So he got up from supper, laid aside his outer clothing, took a towel, and tied it around himself. Next, he poured water into a basin and began to wash his disciples' feet and to dry them with the towel tied around him.

He came to Simon Peter, who asked him, "Lord, are you going to wash my feet?"

Jesus answered him, "What I'm doing you don't realize now, but afterward you will understand."

"You will never wash my feet," Peter said.

Jesus replied, "If I don't wash you, you have no part with me."

Simon Peter said to him, "Lord, not only my feet, but also my hands and my head."

"One who has bathed," Jesus told him, "doesn't need to wash anything except his feet, but he is completely clean. You are clean, but not all of you." For he knew who would betray him. This is why he said, "Not all of you are clean."

When Jesus had washed their feet and put on his outer clothing, he reclined again and said to them, "Do you know what I have done for you? You call me Teacher and Lord—and you are speaking rightly, since that is what I am. So if I, your Lord and Teacher, have washed your feet, you also ought to wash one another's feet. For I have given you an example, that you also should do just as I have done for you.

"Truly I tell you, a servant is not greater than his master, and a messenger is not greater than the one who sent him. If you know these things, you are blessed if you do them.

"I'm not speaking about all of you; I know those I have chosen. But the Scripture must be fulfilled: *The one who eats my bread has raised his heel against me.* I am telling you now before it happens, so that when it does happen you will believe that I am he. Truly I tell you, whoever receives anyone I send receives me, and the one who receives me receives him who sent me."

Someone Will Betray Me

When Jesus had said this, he was troubled in his spirit and testified, "Truly I tell you, one of you will betray me."

The disciples started looking at one another—uncertain which one he was speaking about. They began to argue among themselves which of them it could be who was going to do it.

Deeply distressed, each one began to say to him, "Surely not I, Lord?"

He replied, "The one who dipped his hand with me in the bowl—he will betray me. The Son of Man will go just as it is written about him, but woe to that man by whom the Son of Man is betrayed! It would have been better for him if he had not been born."

Judas, his betrayer, replied, "Surely not I, Rabbi?"

"You have said it," he told him.

One of his disciples, the one Jesus loved, was reclining close beside Jesus. Simon Peter motioned to him to find out who it was he was talking about. So he leaned back against Jesus and asked him, "Lord, who is it?"

Jesus replied, "It is one of the Twelve—he's the one I give the piece of bread to after I have dipped it." When he had dipped the bread, he gave it to Judas, Simon Iscariot's son. After Judas ate the piece of bread, Satan entered him. So Jesus told him, "What you're doing, do quickly."

None of those reclining at the table knew why he said this to him. Since Judas kept the money-bag, some thought that Jesus was telling him, "Buy what we need for the festival," or that he should give something to the poor. After receiving the piece of bread, he immediately left. And it was night.

When he had left, Jesus said, "Now the Son of Man is glorified, and God is glorified in him. If God is glorified in him, God will also glorify him in himself and will glorify him at once. Little children, I am with you a little while longer. You will look for me, and just as I told the Jews, so now I tell you, 'Where I am going, you cannot come.'

"I give you a new command: Love one another. Just as I have loved you, you are also to love one another. By this everyone will know that you are my disciples, if you love one another."

DAY
THIRTY-FOUR

A Terrible Prediction

"Lord," Simon Peter said to him, "where are you going?"

Jesus answered, "Where I am going you cannot follow me now, but you will follow later."

"Lord," Peter asked, "why can't I follow you now? I will lay down my life for you."

Jesus replied, "Will you lay down your life for me?"

Then Jesus said to them, "Tonight all of you will fall away because of me, for it is written:

I will strike the shepherd,
and the sheep of the flock will be scattered.

"But after I have risen, I will go ahead of you to Galilee."

Peter told him, "Even if everyone falls away because of you, I will never fall away."

"Simon, Simon, look out. Satan has asked to sift you like wheat. But I have prayed for you that your faith may not fail. And you, when you have turned back, strengthen your brothers."

"Lord," he told him, "I'm ready to go with you both to prison and to death."

"Truly I tell you," Jesus said to him, "today, this very night, before the rooster crows twice, you will deny me three times."

But he kept insisting, "If I have to die with you, I will never deny you." And they all said the same thing.

He also said to them, "When I sent you out without money-bag, traveling bag, or sandals, did you lack anything?"

"Not a thing," they said.

Then he said to them, "But now, whoever has a money-bag should take it, and also a traveling bag. And whoever doesn't have a sword should sell his robe and buy one. For I tell you, what is written must be fulfilled in me: *And he was counted among the lawless.* Yes, what is written about me is coming to its fulfillment."

"Lord," they said, "look, here are two swords."

"That is enough!" he told them.

The Last Supper

Then he took a cup, and after giving thanks, he said, "Take this and share it among yourselves. For I tell you, from now on I will not drink of the fruit of the vine until the kingdom of God comes."

As they were eating, Jesus took bread, blessed and broke it, gave it to the disciples, and said, "Take and eat it; this is my body which is given for you. Do this in remembrance of me." In the same way he also took the cup after supper, and after giving thanks, he gave it to them and said, "Drink from it, all of you."

And they all drank from it. "For this is my blood of the covenant, which is poured out for many for the forgiveness of sins. But I tell you, I will not drink from this fruit of the vine from now on until that day when I drink it new with you in my Father's kingdom."

Don't Let Your Heart Be Troubled

"Don't let your heart be troubled. Believe in God; believe also in me. In my Father's house are many rooms. If it were not so, would I have told you that I am going to prepare a place for you? If I go away and prepare a place for you, I will come again and take you to myself, so that where I am you may be also. You know the way to where I am going."

"Lord," Thomas said, "we don't know where you're going. How can we know the way?"

Jesus told him, "I am the way, the truth, and the life. No one comes to the Father except through me. If you know me, you will also know my Father. From now on you do know him and have seen him."

"Lord," said Philip, "show us the Father, and that's enough for us."

Jesus said to him, "Have I been among you all this time and you do not know me, Philip? The one who has seen me has seen the Father. How can you say, 'Show us the Father'? Don't you believe that I am in the Father and the Father is in me? The words I speak to you I do not speak on my own. The Father who lives in me does his works. Believe me that I am in the Father and the Father is in me. Otherwise, believe because of the works themselves.

"Truly I tell you, the one who believes in me will also do the works that I do. And he will do even greater works than these, because I am going to the Father. Whatever you ask in my name, I will do it so that the Father may be glorified in the Son. If you ask me anything in my name, I will do it."

If You Love Me

"If you love me, you will keep my commands. And I will ask the Father, and he will give you another Counselor to be with you forever. He is the Spirit of truth. The world is unable to receive him because it doesn't see him or know him. But you do know him, because he remains with you and will be in you.

"I will not leave you as orphans; I am coming to you. In a little while the world will no longer see me, but you will see me. Because I live, you will live too. On that day you will know that I am in my Father, you are in me, and I am in you. The one who has my commands and keeps them is the one who loves me. And the one who loves me will be loved by my Father. I also will love him and will reveal myself to him."

Judas (not Iscariot) said to him, "Lord, how is it you're going to reveal yourself to us and not to the world?"

Jesus answered, "If anyone loves me, he will keep my word. My Father will love him, and we will come to him and make our home with him. The one who doesn't love me will not keep my words. The word that you hear is not mine but is from the Father who sent me.

"I have spoken these things to you while I remain with you. But the Counselor, the Holy Spirit, whom the Father will send in my name, will teach you all things and remind you of everything I have told you.

"Peace I leave with you. My peace I give to you. I do not give to you as the world gives. Don't let your heart be troubled or fearful. You have heard me tell you, 'I am going away and I am coming to you.' If you loved me, you would rejoice that I am going to the Father, because the Father is greater than I. I have told you now before it happens so that when it does happen you may believe. I will not talk with you much longer, because the ruler of the world is coming. He has no power over me. On the contrary, so that the world may know that I love the Father, I do as the Father commanded me.

"Get up; let's leave this place."

Remain in My Love

"I am the true vine, and my Father is the gardener. Every branch in me that does not produce fruit he removes, and he prunes every branch that produces fruit so that it will produce more fruit. You are already clean because of the word I have spoken to you. Remain in me, and I in you. Just as a branch is unable to produce fruit by itself unless it remains on the vine, neither can you unless you remain in me. I am the vine; you are the branches. The one who remains in me and I in him produces much fruit, because you can do nothing without me. If anyone does not remain in me, he is thrown aside like a branch and he withers. They gather them, throw them into the fire, and they are burned. If you remain in me and my words remain in you, ask whatever you want and it will be done for you. My Father is glorified by this: that you produce much fruit and prove to be my disciples.

"As the Father has loved me, I have also loved you. Remain in my love. If you keep my commands you will remain in my love, just as I have kept my Father's commands and remain in his love.

"I have told you these things so that my joy may be in you and your joy may be complete.

"This is my command: Love one another as I have loved you. No one has greater love than this: to lay down his life for his friends. You are my friends if you do what I command you. I do not call you servants anymore, because a servant doesn't know what his master is doing. I have called you friends, because I have made known to you everything I have heard from my Father. You did not choose me, but I chose you. I appointed you to go and produce fruit and that your fruit should remain, so that whatever you ask the Father in my name, he will give you.

"This is what I command you: Love one another."

DAY
THIRTY-FIVE

Expect Opposition

"If the world hates you, understand that it hated me before it hated you. If you were of the world, the world would love you as its own. However, because you are not of the world, but I have chosen you out of it, the world hates you. Remember the word I spoke to you: 'A servant is not greater than his master.' If they persecuted me, they will also persecute you. If they kept my word, they will also keep yours. But they will do all these things to you on account of my name, because they don't know the one who sent me. If I had not come and spoken to them, they would not be guilty of sin. Now they have no excuse for their sin. The one who hates me also hates my Father. If I had not done the works among them that no one else has done, they would not be guilty of sin. Now they have seen and hated both me and my Father. But this happened so that the statement written in their law might be fulfilled: *They hated me for no reason.*

"When the Counselor comes, the one I will send to you from the Father—the Spirit of truth who proceeds from the Father—he will testify about me. You also will testify, because you have been with me from the beginning.

"I have told you these things to keep you from stumbling. They will ban you from the synagogues. In fact, a time is coming when anyone who kills you will think he is offering service to God. They will do these things because they haven't known the Father or me. But I have told you these things so that when their time comes you will remember I told them to you. I didn't tell you these things from the beginning, because I was with you."

The Spirit of Truth

"But now I am going away to him who sent me, and not one of you asks me, 'Where are you going?' Yet, because I have spoken these things to you, sorrow has filled your heart. Nevertheless, I am telling you the truth. It is for your benefit that I go away, because if I don't go away the Counselor will not come to you. If I go, I will send him to you. When he comes, he will convict the world about sin, righteousness, and judgment: About sin, because they do not believe in me; about righteousness, because I am going to the Father and you will no longer see me; and about judgment, because the ruler of this world has been judged.

"I still have many things to tell you, but you can't bear them now. When the Spirit of truth comes, he will guide you into all the truth. For he will not speak on his own, but he will speak whatever he hears. He will also declare to you what is to come. He will glorify me, because he will take from what is mine and declare it to you. Everything the Father has is mine. This is why I told you that he takes from what is mine and will declare it to you."

A Promise of Joy

"In a little while, you will no longer see me; again in a little while, you will see me."

Then some of his disciples said to one another, "What is this he's telling us: 'In a little while, you will not see me; again in a little while, you will see me,' and, 'Because I am going to the Father'?" They said, "What is this he is saying, 'In a little while'? We don't know what he's talking about."

Jesus knew they wanted to ask him, and so he said to them, "Are you asking one another about what I said, 'In a little while, you will not see me; again in a little while, you will see me'? Truly I tell you, you will weep and mourn, but the world will rejoice. You will become sorrowful, but your sorrow will turn to joy. When a woman is in labor, she has pain because her time has come. But when she has given birth to a child, she no longer remembers the suffering because of the joy that a person has been born into the world. So you also have sorrow now. But I will see you again. Your hearts will rejoice, and no one will take away your joy from you."

A Promise of Answered Prayer and Peace

"In that day you will not ask me anything. Truly I tell you, anything you ask the Father in my name, he will give you. Until now you have asked for nothing in my name. Ask and you will receive, so that your joy may be complete.

"I have spoken these things to you in figures of speech. A time is coming when I will no longer speak to you in figures, but I will tell you plainly about the Father. On that day you will ask in my name, and I am not telling you that I will ask the Father on your behalf. For the Father himself loves you, because you have loved me and have believed that I came from God. I came from the Father and have come into the world. Again, I am leaving the world and going to the Father."

His disciples said, "Look, now you're speaking plainly and not using any figurative language. Now we know that you know everything and don't need anyone to question you. By this we believe that you came from God."

Jesus responded to them, "Do you now believe? Indeed, an hour is coming, and has come, when each of you will be scattered to his own home, and you will leave me alone. Yet I am not alone, because the Father is with me. I have told you these things so that in me you may have peace. You will have suffering in this world. Be courageous! I have conquered the world."

Jesus Prays

Jesus spoke these things, looked up to heaven, and said, "Father, the hour has come. Glorify your Son so that the Son may glorify you, since you gave him authority over all people, so that he may give eternal life to everyone you have given him. This is eternal life: that they may know you, the only true God, and the one you have sent—Jesus Christ. I have glorified you on the earth by completing the work you gave me to do. Now, Father, glorify me in your presence with that glory I had with you before the world existed.

"I have revealed your name to the people you gave me from the world. They were yours, you gave them to me, and they have kept your word. Now they know that everything you have given me is from you, because I have given them the words you gave me. They have received them and have known for certain that I came from you. They have believed that you sent me.

"I pray for them. I am not praying for the world but for those you have given me, because they are yours. Everything I have is yours, and everything you have is mine, and I am glorified in them. I am no longer in the world, but they are in the world, and I am coming to you. Holy Father, protect them by your name that you have given me, so that they may be one as we are one. While I was with them, I was protecting them by your name that you have given me. I guarded them and not one of them is lost, except the son of destruction, so that the Scripture may be fulfilled. Now I am coming to you, and I speak these things in the world so that they may have my joy completed in them. I have given them your word. The world hated them because they are not of the world, just as I am not of the world. I am not praying that you take them out of the world but that you protect them from the evil one. They are not of the world, just as I am not of the world. Sanctify them by the truth; your word is truth. As you sent me into the world, I also have sent them into the world. I sanctify myself for them, so that they also may be sanctified by the truth.

"I pray not only for these, but also for those who believe in me through their word. May they all be one, as you, Father, are in me and I am in you. May they also be in us, so that the world may believe you sent me. I have given them the glory you have given me, so that they may be one as we are one. I am in them and you are in me, so that they may be made completely one, that the world may know you have sent me and have loved them as you have loved me.

"Father, I want those you have given me to be with me where I am, so that they will see my glory, which you have given me because you loved me before the world's foundation. Righteous Father, the world has not known you. However, I have known you, and they have known that you sent me. I made your name known to them and will continue to make it known, so that the love you have loved me with may be in them and I may be in them."

In the Garden of Gethsemane

After Jesus had said these things and after singing a hymn, he went out with his disciples across the Kidron Valley to the Mount of Olives where there was a garden.

They came to a place called Gethsemane, and he told the disciples, "Pray that you may not fall into temptation. Sit here while I go over there and pray." Taking along Peter and the two sons of Zebedee, James and John, he began to be deeply distressed and troubled. He said to them, "I am deeply grieved to the point of death. Remain here and stay awake with me."

Going a little farther he withdrew from them about a stone's throw. He knelt and fell facedown and prayed, "*Abba*, Father! All things are possible for you. My Father, if you are willing, let this cup pass from me. Yet not as I will, but as you will."

Then an angel from heaven appeared to him, strengthening him. Being in anguish, he prayed more fervently, and his sweat became like drops of blood falling to the ground.

Then he came to the disciples and found them sleeping. He asked Peter, "Simon, why are you sleeping? Couldn't you stay awake with me one hour? Stay awake and pray, so that you won't enter into temptation. The spirit is willing, but the flesh is weak."

Again, a second time, he went away and prayed, "My Father, if this cannot pass unless I drink it, your will be done." And he came again and found them sleeping, because they could not keep their eyes open. They did not know what to say to him.

After leaving them, he went away again and prayed a third time, saying the same thing once more. Then he came to the disciples, and he found them sleeping again, exhausted from their grief. He said to them, "Are you still sleeping and resting? Enough! See, the time is near. The Son of Man is betrayed into the hands of sinners. Get up; let's go. See, my betrayer is near."

Betrayed and Arrested

While Jesus was still speaking, Judas, one of the Twelve, suddenly arrived. Judas knew the place because Jesus often met there with his disciples. With him was a large mob, including a company of soldiers and some officials from the chief priests, Pharisees, scribes, and the elders, with lanterns, torches, swords, and clubs.

The betrayer had given them a signal. "The one I kiss," he said, "he's the one; arrest him and take him away under guard." So when he came, immediately he went up to Jesus and said, "Greetings, Rabbi!" and kissed him. Jesus said to him, "Judas, are you betraying the Son of Man with a kiss?"

Jesus, knowing everything that was about to happen to him, went out and said to them, "Who is it that you're seeking?"

"Jesus of Nazareth," they answered.

"I am he," Jesus told them.

Judas, who betrayed him, was also standing with them. When Jesus told them, "I am he," they stepped back and fell to the ground.

Then he asked them again, "Who is it that you're seeking?"

"Jesus of Nazareth," they said.

"I told you I am he," Jesus replied. "So if you're looking for me, let these men go." This was to fulfill the words he had said: "I have not lost one of those you have given me."

Then they came up, took hold of Jesus, and arrested him. When those around him saw what was going to happen, they asked, "Lord, should we strike with the sword?"

Then Simon Peter, who had a sword, drew it, struck the high priest's servant, and cut off his right ear. (The servant's name was Malchus.)

At that, Jesus said to Peter, "No more of this! Put your sword away because all who take up the sword will perish by the sword! Am I not to drink the cup the Father has given me? Or do you think that I cannot call on my Father, and he will provide me here and now with more than twelve legions of angels? How, then, would the Scriptures be fulfilled that say it must happen this way?" And touching his ear, he healed him.

Then Jesus said to the chief priests, temple police, and the elders who had come for him, "Have you come out with swords and clubs as if I were a criminal? Every day while I was with you in the temple, you never laid a hand on me. But this is your hour—and the dominion of darkness."

But all this has happened so that the writings of the prophets would be fulfilled.

Then all the disciples deserted him and ran away. Now a certain young man, wearing nothing but a linen cloth, was following him. They caught hold of him, but he left the linen cloth behind and ran away naked.

Then the company of soldiers, the commander, and the Jewish officials arrested Jesus and tied him up.

Trial—Jewish Phase One (Annas)

First they led him to Annas, since he was the father-in-law of Caiaphas, who was high priest that year. Caiaphas was the one who had advised the Jews that it would be better for one man to die for the people.

The high priest questioned Jesus about his disciples and about his teaching.

"I have spoken openly to the world," Jesus answered him. "I have always taught in the synagogue and in the temple, where all the Jews gather, and I haven't spoken anything in secret. Why do you question me? Question those who heard what I told them. Look, they know what I said."

When he had said these things, one of the officials standing by slapped Jesus, saying, "Is this the way you answer the high priest?"

"If I have spoken wrongly," Jesus answered him, "give evidence about the wrong; but if rightly, why do you hit me?" Then Annas sent him bound to Caiaphas the high priest. They seized him, led him away, and brought him into the high priest's house, where the scribes and the elders had convened.

Peter in the Courtyard

Simon Peter was following Jesus at a distance right to the high priest's courtyard, as was another disciple. That disciple was an acquaintance of the high priest; so he went with Jesus into the high priest's courtyard. But Peter remained standing outside by the door.

Now the servants and the officials had made a charcoal fire, because it was cold. They were standing there warming themselves in the middle of the courtyard, and Peter was standing with them, to see the outcome.

Trial — Jewish Phase Two (Caiaphas)

The chief priests and the whole Sanhedrin were looking for false testimony against Jesus to put him to death, but they could not find any. For many were giving false testimony against him, and the testimonies did not agree. Finally, two who came forward stated, "We heard him say, 'I will destroy this temple made with human hands, and in three days I will build another not made by hands.'" Yet their testimony did not agree even on this.

The high priest stood up and said to him, "Don't you have an answer to what these men are testifying against you?" But Jesus kept silent and did not answer. Again, the high priest said to him, "I charge you under oath by the living God: Tell us if you are the Messiah, the Son of God. Are you the Messiah, the Son of the Blessed One?"

"You have said it," Jesus told him. "I am. But I tell you, in the future you will see the Son of Man seated at the right hand of Power and coming on the clouds of heaven."

Then the high priest tore his robes and said, "He has blasphemed! Why do we still need witnesses? See, now you have heard the blasphemy. What is your decision?"

They answered, "He deserves death!" They all condemned him as deserving death. Some spat in his face and beat him. The men who were holding Jesus started mocking him. Temple servants slapped him. After blindfolding him, they kept asking, "Prophesy! Who was it that hit you?" And they were saying many other blasphemous things to him.

Peter Denies That He Knows Jesus

So the other disciple, the one known to the high priest, went out and spoke to the girl who was the doorkeeper and brought Peter in. When she saw Peter she looked closely at him and said, "This man was with him too. You also were with Jesus, the man from Nazareth."

But he denied it in front of everyone: "Woman, I don't know him. I don't know or understand what you're talking about." Then he went out to the entry-way, and a rooster crowed.

When the maidservant saw him again, she began to tell those standing nearby, "This man is one of them with Jesus the Nazarene."

And again, he denied it with an oath: "I don't know the man!"

About an hour later, those standing there approached Peter and another kept insisting, "This man was certainly with him, since he's also a Galilean. You really are one of them, since even your accent gives you away."

One of the high priest's servants, a relative of the man whose ear Peter had cut off, said, "Didn't I see you with him in the garden?"

Then Peter started to curse and swear, "I don't know this man you're talking about!"

Immediately a rooster crowed a second time.

Then the Lord turned and looked at Peter. So Peter remembered the word of the Lord, how he had said to him, "Before the rooster crows today twice, you will deny me three times." And he went outside, broke down, and wept bitterly.

Trial — Jewish Phase Three (Sanhedrin)

When daylight came, the elders of the people, both the chief priests and the scribes, convened and brought him before their Sanhedrin. They said, "If you are the Messiah, tell us."

But he said to them, "If I do tell you, you will not believe. And if I ask you, you will not answer. But from now on, the Son of Man will be seated at the right hand of the power of God."

They all asked, "Are you, then, the Son of God?"

And he said to them, "You say that I am."

"Why do we need any more testimony," they said, "since we've heard it ourselves from his mouth?"

The End of Judas

Then Judas, his betrayer, seeing that Jesus had been condemned, was full of remorse and returned the thirty pieces of silver to the chief priests and elders. "I have sinned by betraying innocent blood," he said.

"What's that to us?" they said. "See to it yourself!" So he threw the silver into the temple and departed. Then he went and hanged himself.

The chief priests took the silver and said, "It's not permitted to put it into the temple treasury, since it is blood money." They conferred together and bought the potter's field with it as a burial place for foreigners. Therefore that field has been called "Field of Blood" to this day. Then what was spoken through the prophet Jeremiah was fulfilled: "They took the thirty pieces of silver, the price of him whose price was set by the Israelites, and they gave them for the potter's field, as the Lord directed me."

DAY
THIRTY-SEVEN

Trial—Roman Phase One (Pilate)

Then their whole assembly rose, tied Jesus up, and led him from Caiaphas to Pilate the governor, at the governor's headquarters. It was early morning. They did not enter the headquarters themselves; otherwise they would be defiled and unable to eat the Passover.

So Pilate came out to them and said, "What charge do you bring against this man?"

They answered him, "If this man weren't a criminal, we wouldn't have handed him over to you."

Pilate told them, "You take him and judge him according to your law."

"It's not legal for us to put anyone to death," the Jews declared. They said this so that Jesus's words might be fulfilled indicating what kind of death he was going to die.

They began to accuse him, saying, "We found this man misleading our nation, opposing payment of taxes to Caesar, and saying that he himself is the Messiah, a king."

While he was being accused by the chief priests and elders, Jesus didn't answer. Then Pilate said to him,

"Aren't you going to answer? Don't you hear how much they are testifying against you? Look how many things they are accusing you of!" But he didn't answer him on even one charge, so that the governor was quite amazed.

Then Pilate went back into the headquarters, summoned Jesus, and said to him, "Are you the king of the Jews?"

Jesus answered, "Are you asking this on your own, or have others told you about me?"

"I'm not a Jew, am I?" Pilate replied. "Your own nation and the chief priests handed you over to me. What have you done?"

"My kingdom is not of this world," said Jesus. "If my kingdom were of this world, my servants would fight, so that I wouldn't be handed over to the Jews. But as it is, my kingdom is not from here."

"You are a king then?" Pilate asked.

"You say that I'm a king," Jesus replied. "I was born for this, and I have come into the world for this: to testify to the truth. Everyone who is of the truth listens to my voice."

"What is truth?" said Pilate.

After he had said this, he went out to the Jews again and told them, "I find no grounds for charging him."

But they kept insisting, "He stirs up the people, teaching throughout all Judea, from Galilee where he started even to here."

Trial — Roman Phase Two (Herod Antipas)

When Pilate heard this, he asked if the man was a Galilean. Finding that he was under Herod's jurisdiction, he sent him to Herod, who was also in Jerusalem during those days. Herod was very glad to see Jesus; for a long time he had wanted to see him because he had heard about him and was hoping to see some miracle performed by him. So he kept asking him questions, but Jesus did not answer him. The chief priests and the scribes stood by, vehemently accusing him. Then Herod, with his soldiers, treated him with contempt, mocked him, dressed him in bright clothing, and sent him back to Pilate. That very day Herod and Pilate became friends. Previously, they had been enemies.

Trial — Roman Phase Three (Pilate)

Pilate called together the chief priests, the leaders, and the people, and said to them, "You have brought me this man as one who misleads the people. But in fact, after examining him in your presence, I have found no grounds to charge this man with those things you accuse him of. Neither has Herod, because he sent him back to us. Clearly, he has done nothing to deserve death. Therefore, I will have him whipped and then release him."

At the festival the governor's custom was to release to the crowd a prisoner they wanted. At that time they had a notorious prisoner called Barabbas, who was in prison with rebels who had committed murder during the rebellion. The crowd came up and began to ask Pilate to do for them as was his custom. Pilate answered them, "Who is it you want me to release for you—Barabbas, or Jesus, the king of the Jews?" For he knew it was because of envy that the chief priests had handed him over.

While he was sitting on the judge's bench, his wife sent word to him, "Have nothing to do with that righteous man, for today I've suffered terribly in a dream because of him."

The chief priests and the elders, however, persuaded and stirred up the crowds to ask for Barabbas and to execute Jesus. The governor asked them, "Which of the two do you want me to release for you?" Then they all cried out together, "Take this man away! Release Barabbas to us!"

Wanting to release Jesus, Pilate addressed them again, "What should I do then with Jesus, who is called Christ?" But they kept shouting, "Crucify! Crucify him!"

A third time he said to them, "Why? What has this man done wrong? I have found in him no grounds for the death penalty. Therefore, I will have him whipped and then release him." But they shouted all the more, "Crucify him!"

Then Pilate took Jesus and had him flogged. The governor's soldiers took Jesus into the governor's residence and gathered the whole company around him. The soldiers twisted together a crown of thorns, put it on his head. They stripped him, clothed him in a purple robe, and placed a staff in his right hand. They mocked him by getting on their knees and paying him homage. They kept coming up to him and saying, "Hail, king of the Jews!" They were hitting him on the head with a stick, spitting on him, and slapping his face.

Pilate went outside again and said to them, "Look, I'm bringing him out to you to let you know I find no grounds for charging him." Then Jesus came out wearing the crown of thorns and the purple robe. Pilate said to them, "Here is the man!"

When the chief priests and the temple servants saw him, they shouted, "Crucify! Crucify!"

Pilate responded, "Take him and crucify him yourselves, since I find no grounds for charging him."

"We have a law," the Jews replied to him, "and according to that law he ought to die, because he made himself the Son of God."

When Pilate heard this statement, he was more afraid than ever. He went back into the headquarters and asked Jesus, "Where are you from?" But Jesus did not give him an answer. So Pilate said to him, "Do you refuse to speak to me? Don't you know that I have the authority to release you and the authority to crucify you?"

"You would have no authority over me at all," Jesus answered him, "if it hadn't been given you from above. This is why the one who handed me over to you has the greater sin."

From that moment Pilate kept trying to release him. But the Jews shouted, "If you release this man, you are not Caesar's friend. Anyone who makes himself a king opposes Caesar!" They kept up the pressure, demanding with loud voices that he be crucified.

When Pilate heard these words, he brought Jesus outside. He sat down on the judge's seat in a place called the Stone Pavement (but in Aramaic, *Gabbatha*). It was the preparation day for the Passover, and it was about noon. Then he told the Jews, "Here is your king!"

They shouted, "Take him away! Take him away! Crucify him!"

Pilate said to them, "Should I crucify your king?"

"We have no king but Caesar!" the chief priests answered and their voices won out.

When Pilate saw that he was getting nowhere, but that a riot was starting instead, he took some water, washed his hands in front of the crowd, and said, "I am innocent of this man's blood. See to it yourselves!"

All the people answered, "His blood be on us and on our children!"

So Pilate decided to grant their demand and released Barabbas. Then he handed Jesus over to be crucified.

The Road to Golgotha

After they had mocked Jesus, they stripped him of the purple robe, put his own clothes on him, and led him away carrying the cross by himself to crucify him.

As they were going out, they forced a man coming in from the country, who was passing by, to carry Jesus's cross. He was Simon of Cyrene, the father of Alexander and Rufus. They laid the cross on him to carry behind Jesus.

A large crowd of people followed him, including women who were mourning and lamenting him. But turning to them, Jesus said, "Daughters of Jerusalem, do not weep for me, but weep for yourselves and your children. Look, the days are coming when they will say, 'Blessed are the women without children, the wombs that never bore, and the breasts that never nursed!' Then they will begin to say to the mountains, 'Fall on us!' and to the hills, 'Cover us!' For if they do these things when the wood is green, what will happen when it is dry?"

They brought Jesus to Place of the Skull, which in Aramaic is called *Golgotha*. They tried to give him wine mixed with myrrh, but he did not take it.

DAY
THIRTY-EIGHT

Jesus Is Crucified

There they crucified him and two others—criminals—with him, one on either side, with Jesus in the middle. Now it was nine in the morning when they crucified him.

Jesus said, "Father, forgive them, because they do not know what they are doing."

Pilate also had a sign made and put on the cross above his head. It said: THIS IS JESUS OF NAZARETH, THE KING OF THE JEWS. Many of the Jews read this sign, because the place where Jesus was crucified was near the city, and it was written in Aramaic, Latin, and Greek. So the chief priests of the Jews said to Pilate, "Don't write, 'The king of the Jews,' but that he said, 'I am the king of the Jews.'"

Pilate replied, "What I have written, I have written."

When the soldiers crucified Jesus, they took his clothes and divided them into four parts, a part for each soldier. They also took the tunic, which was seamless, woven in one piece from the top. So they said to one another, "Let's not tear it, but cast lots for it, to see who gets it." This happened that the Scripture might be fulfilled that says: *They divided my clothes among them-selves, and they cast lots for my clothing.* This is what the soldiers did. Then they sat down and were guarding him there.

Those who passed by were yelling insults at him, shaking their heads and saying, "You who would destroy the temple and rebuild it in three days, save yourself! If you are the Son of God, come down from the cross, save yourself!" In the same way the chief priests, with the scribes and elders, mocked him and said, "He saved others, but he cannot save himself! He is the King of Israel! Let him come down now from the cross, and we will believe in him. He trusts in God; let God rescue him now—if he takes pleasure in him! For he said, 'I am the Son of God.'" The soldiers also mocked him. They came offering him sour wine and said, "If you are the king of the Jews, save yourself!"

In the same way even the criminals who were crucified with him taunted him. One of the criminals hanging there began to yell insults at him: "Aren't you the Messiah? Save yourself and us!"

But the other answered, rebuking him: "Don't you even fear God, since you are undergoing the same punishment? We are punished justly, because we're get-ting back what we deserve for the things we did, but this man has done nothing wrong." Then he said, "Jesus, remember me when you come into your kingdom."

And he said to him, "Truly I tell you, today you will be with me in paradise."

It was now about noon. Standing by the cross of Jesus were his mother, his mother's sister, Mary the wife of Clopas, and Mary Magdalene. When Jesus saw his mother and the disciple he loved standing there, he said to his mother, "Woman, here is your son." Then he said to the disciple, "Here is your mother." And from that hour the disciple took her into his home.

It Is Finished

From noon until three in the afternoon, darkness came over the whole land because the sun's light failed. About three in the afternoon Jesus cried out with a loud voice, *"Eloi, Eloi, lemá sabachtháni?"* which is translated, "My God, my God, why have you abandoned me?"

When some of those standing there heard this, they said, "See, he's calling for Elijah."

After this, when Jesus knew that everything was now finished that the Scripture might be fulfilled, he said, "I'm thirsty." A jar full of sour wine was sitting there; so they fixed a sponge full of sour wine on a hyssop branch and held it up to his mouth and said, "Let's see if Elijah comes to take him down."

When Jesus had received the sour wine, he said, "It is finished." And Jesus called out with a loud voice, "Father, *into your hands I entrust my spirit.*" Bowing his head, he gave up his spirit and breathed his last.

Supernatural Events

Suddenly, the curtain of the sanctuary was torn in two from top to bottom, the earth quaked, and the rocks were split. The tombs were also opened and many bodies of the saints who had fallen asleep were raised. And they came out of the tombs after his resurrection, entered the holy city, and appeared to many.

When the centurion and those with him, who were keeping watch over Jesus, saw the earthquake and the things that had happened, they were terrified and said, "Truly this man was the Son of God!"

All the crowds that had gathered for this spectacle, when they saw what had taken place, went home, striking their chests.

But all who knew him, including many women who had followed Jesus from Galilee and looked after him, were there, watching from a distance. Among them were Mary Magdalene, Mary the mother of James the younger and of Joses, and Salome the mother of Zebedee's sons.

The Death of Jesus Confirmed

Since it was the preparation day, the Jews did not want the bodies to remain on the cross on the Sabbath (for that Sabbath was a special day). They requested that Pilate have the men's legs broken and that their bodies be taken away. So the soldiers came and broke the legs of the first man and of the other one who had been crucified with him. When they came to Jesus, they did not break his legs since they saw that he was already dead. But one of the soldiers pierced his side with a spear, and at once blood and water came out. He who saw this has testified so that you also may believe. His testimony is true, and he knows he is telling the truth. For these things happened so that the Scripture would be fulfilled:

"Not one of his bones will be broken."

Also, another Scripture says:

"They will look at the one they pierced."

The Burial of Jesus

When it was already evening, because it was the day of preparation (that is, the day before the Sabbath), Joseph of Arimathea, a prominent member of the Sanhedrin, a good and righteous man, who had not agreed with their plan and action, and who was himself looking forward to the kingdom of God, came and boldly went to Pilate and asked for Jesus's body. Pilate was surprised that he was already dead. Summoning the centurion, he asked him whether he had already died. When he found out from the centurion, Pilate gave him permission. He gave the corpse to Joseph who came and took the body away.

Nicodemus (who had previously come to him at night) also came, bringing a mixture of about seventy-five pounds of myrrh and aloes. They took Jesus's body and wrapped it in clean, fine linen cloths with the fragrant spices, according to the burial custom of the Jews. There was a garden in the place where he was crucified. In it was a tomb Joseph had newly cut into the rock, where no one had ever been placed. They placed Jesus there because of the Jewish day of preparation and since the tomb was nearby. He left after rolling a great stone against the entrance of the tomb.

It was the preparation day, and the Sabbath was about to begin. The women who had come with him from Galilee followed: Mary Magdalene and the other Mary, the mother of Joses. They were seated there, facing the tomb, and observed where and how his body was placed. Then they returned and prepared spices and perfumes. And they rested on the Sabbath according to the commandment.

The Tomb Is Sealed

The next day, which followed the preparation day, the chief priests and the Pharisees gathered before Pilate and said, "Sir, we remember that while this deceiver was still alive he said, 'After three days I will rise again.' So give orders that the tomb be made secure until the third day. Otherwise, his disciples may come, steal him, and tell the people, 'He has been raised from the dead,' and the last deception will be worse than the first."

"Take guards," Pilate told them. "Go and make it as secure as you know how." They went and secured the tomb by setting a seal on the stone and placing the guards.

DAY
THIRTY-NINE

The Empty Tomb

When the Sabbath was over, on the first day of the week, Mary Magdalene, Joanna, Mary the mother of James, and Salome bought spices, so that they could go and anoint him.

There was a violent earthquake, because an angel of the Lord descended from heaven and approached the tomb. He rolled back the stone and was sitting on it. His appearance was like lightning, and his clothing was as white as snow. The guards were so shaken by fear of him that they became like dead men.

Mary Magdalene came to the tomb early, while it was still dark. She saw that the stone had been removed from the tomb. So she went running to Simon Peter and to the other disciple, the one Jesus loved, and said to them, "They've taken the Lord out of the tomb, and we don't know where they've put him!"

As it was dawning at sunrise, the other Mary, Salome, and other women came to the tomb, bringing the spices they had prepared. They were saying to one another, "Who will roll away the stone from the entrance to the tomb for us?" But they noticed that the stone—which was very large—had been rolled away from the tomb.

They went in but did not find the body of the Lord Jesus. While they were perplexed about this, suddenly two men stood by them in dazzling clothes. So the women were terrified and bowed down to the ground.

The angel dressed in a white robe sitting on the right side told the women, "Don't be afraid, because I know you are looking for Jesus of Nazareth who was crucified. Why are you looking for the living among the dead? He is not here, but he has risen! Come and see the place where he lay. Then go quickly and tell his disciples and Peter, 'He has risen from the dead and indeed he is going ahead of you to Galilee; you will see him there just as he told you.' Listen, I have told you.

"Remember how he spoke to you when he was still in Galilee, saying, 'It is necessary that the Son of Man be betrayed into the hands of sinful men, be crucified, and rise on the third day'?" And they remembered his words.

They went out and ran from the tomb with fear and great joy, because trembling and astonishment overwhelmed them. And they said nothing to anyone, since they were afraid. Returning from the tomb, they went running to tell his disciples the news.

Peter and John See the Empty Tomb

Peter and the other disciple went out, heading for the tomb. The two were running together, but the other disciple outran Peter and got to the tomb first. Stooping down, he saw the linen cloths lying there, but he did not go in. Then, following him, Simon Peter also came. He entered the tomb and saw only the linen cloths lying there. The wrapping that had been on his head was not lying with the linen cloths but was folded up in a separate place by itself. The other disciple, who had reached the tomb first, then also went in, saw, and believed. Peter went away, amazed at what had happened. For they did not yet understand the Scripture that he must rise from the dead. Then the disciples returned to the place where they were staying, amazed at what had happened.

Jesus Appears to Mary Magdalene

Mary Magdalene stood outside the tomb, crying. As she was crying, she stooped to look into the tomb. She saw two angels in white sitting where Jesus's body had been lying, one at the head and the other at the feet. They said to her, "Woman, why are you crying?"

"Because they've taken away my Lord," she told them, "and I don't know where they've put him."

Having said this, she turned around and saw Jesus standing there, but she did not know it was Jesus.

"Woman," Jesus said to her, "why are you crying? Who is it that you're seeking?"

Supposing he was the gardener, she replied, "Sir, if you've carried him away, tell me where you've put him, and I will take him away."

Jesus said to her, "Mary."

Turning around, she said to him in Aramaic, *"Rabboni!"*—which means "Teacher."

"Don't cling to me," Jesus told her, "since I have not yet ascended to the Father. But go to my brothers and tell them that I am ascending to my Father and your Father, to my God and your God."

Mary Magdalene went and reported to the disciples, as they were mourning and weeping. She announced, "I have seen the Lord!" Yet, when they heard that he was alive, had been seen by her, and what she said to her, they did not believe it.

Jesus Appears to the Other Women

The other women were returning from the tomb to tell the disciples. Just then Jesus met them and said, "Greetings!" They came up, took hold of his feet, and worshiped him. Then Jesus told them, "Do not be afraid. Go and tell my brothers to leave for Galilee, and they will see me there."

They went and told all these things to the Eleven and to all the rest. But these words seemed like nonsense to them, and they did not believe the women.

The Soldiers Report to the Jewish Authorities

As they were on their way, some of the guards came into the city and reported to the chief priests everything that had happened. After the priests had assembled with the elders and agreed on a plan, they gave the soldiers a large sum of money and told them, "Say this, 'His disciples came during the night and stole him while we were sleeping.' If this reaches the governor's ears, we will deal with him and keep you out of trouble." They took the money and did as they were instructed, and this story has been spread among Jewish people to this day.

Appearance on the Road to Emmaus

Now that same day two of them were on their way to a village called Emmaus, which was about seven miles from Jerusalem. Together they were discussing everything that had taken place. And while they were discussing and arguing, Jesus himself came near and began to walk along with them. But they were prevented from recognizing him as he appeared in a different form. Then he asked them, "What is this dispute that you're having with each other as you are walking?" And they stopped walking and looked discouraged.

The one named Cleopas answered him, "Are you the only visitor in Jerusalem who doesn't know the things that happened there in these days?"

"What things?" he asked them.

So they said to him, "The things concerning Jesus of Nazareth, who was a prophet powerful in action and speech before God and all the people, and how our chief priests and leaders handed him over to be sentenced to death, and they crucified him. But we were hoping that he was the one who was about to redeem Israel. Besides all this, it's the third day since these things happened. Moreover, some women from our group astounded us. They arrived early at the tomb, and when they didn't find his body, they came and reported that they had seen a vision of angels who said he was alive. Some of those who were with us went to the tomb and found it just as the women had said, but they didn't see him."

He said to them, "How foolish you are, and how slow to believe all that the prophets have spoken! Wasn't it necessary for the Messiah to suffer these things and enter into his glory?" Then beginning with Moses and all the Prophets, he interpreted for them the things concerning himself in all the Scriptures.

They came near the village where they were going, and he gave the impression that he was going farther. But they urged him, "Stay with us, because it's almost evening, and now the day is almost over." So he went in to stay with them.

It was as he reclined at the table with them that he took the bread, blessed and broke it, and gave it to them. Then their eyes were opened, and they recognized him, but he disappeared from their sight. They said to each other, "Weren't our hearts burning within us while he was talking with us on the road and explaining the Scriptures to us?" That very hour they got up and returned to Jerusalem. They found the Eleven and those with them gathered together, who said, "The Lord has truly been raised and has appeared to Simon!" Then they began to describe what had happened on the road and how he was made known to them in the breaking of the bread. Those gathered did not believe them either.

DAY
FORTY

Appearance in the Upper Room

As they were saying these things, Jesus himself stood in their midst. It was evening on that first day of the week, and the disciples were gathered together with the doors locked because they feared the Jews.

He said to them, "Peace to you!" But they were startled and terrified and thought they were seeing a ghost. "Why are you troubled?" he asked them. "And why do doubts arise in your hearts? Look at my hands and my feet, that it is I myself! Touch me and see, because a ghost does not have flesh and bones as you can see I have." Having said this, he showed them his hands and feet.

But while they still were amazed and in disbelief because of their joy, he asked them, "Do you have anything here to eat?" So they gave him a piece of a broiled fish, and he took it and ate in their presence. So the disciples rejoiced when they saw the Lord.

Jesus said to them again, "Peace be with you. As the Father has sent me, I also send you." After saying this, he breathed on them and said, "Receive the Holy

Spirit. If you forgive the sins of any, they are forgiven them; if you retain the sins of any, they are retained."

He told them, "These are my words that I spoke to you while I was still with you—that everything written about me in the Law of Moses, the Prophets, and the Psalms must be fulfilled." Then he opened their minds to understand the Scriptures. He also said to them, "This is what is written: The Messiah will suffer and rise from the dead the third day, and repentance for forgiveness of sins will be proclaimed in his name to all the nations, beginning at Jerusalem. You are witnesses of these things. And look, I am sending you what my Father promised. As for you, stay in the city until you are empowered from on high."

Thomas Sees and Believes

But Thomas (called "Twin"), one of the Twelve, was not with them when Jesus came. So the other disciples were telling him, "We've seen the Lord!"

But he said to them, "If I don't see the mark of the nails in his hands, put my finger into the mark of the nails, and put my hand into his side, I will never believe."

A week later his disciples were indoors again, and Thomas was with them. Even though the doors were locked, Jesus came and stood among them and said, "Peace be with you."

Then he said to Thomas, "Put your finger here and look at my hands. Reach out your hand and put it into my side. Don't be faithless, but believe."

Thomas responded to him, "My Lord and my God!"

Jesus said, "Because you have seen me, you have believed. Blessed are those who have not seen and yet believe."

Appearance to Disciples by the Sea

After this, Jesus revealed himself again to his disciples by the Sea of Tiberias. He revealed himself in this way:

Simon Peter, Thomas (called "Twin"), Nathanael from Cana of Galilee, Zebedee's sons, and two others of his disciples were together.

"I'm going fishing," Simon Peter said to them.

"We're coming with you," they told him. They went out and got into the boat, but that night they caught nothing.

When daybreak came, Jesus stood on the shore, but the disciples did not know it was Jesus. "Friends," Jesus called to them, "you don't have any fish, do you?"

"No," they answered.

"Cast the net on the right side of the boat," he told them, "and you'll find some." So they did, and they were unable to haul it in because of the large number of fish. The disciple, the one Jesus loved, said to Peter, "It is the Lord!"

When Simon Peter heard that it was the Lord, he tied his outer clothing around him (for he had taken it off) and plunged into the sea. Since they were not far from land (about a hundred yards away), the other disciples came in the boat, dragging the net full of fish.

When they got out on land, they saw a charcoal fire there, with fish lying on it, and bread. "Bring some of the fish you've just caught," Jesus told them. So Simon Peter climbed up and hauled the net ashore, full of large fish—153 of them. Even though there were so many, the net was not torn.

"Come and have breakfast," Jesus told them. None of the disciples dared ask him, "Who are you?" because they knew it was the Lord. Jesus came, took the bread, and gave it to them. He did the same with the fish. This was now the third time Jesus appeared to the disciples after he was raised from the dead.

When they had eaten breakfast, Jesus asked Simon Peter, "Simon, son of John, do you love me more than these?"

"Yes, Lord," he said to him, "you know that I love you."

"Feed my lambs," he told him.

A second time he asked him, "Simon, son of John, do you love me?"

"Yes, Lord," he said to him, "you know that I love you."

"Shepherd my sheep," he told him.

He asked him the third time, "Simon, son of John, do you love me?"

Peter was grieved that he asked him the third time, "Do you love me?" He said, "Lord, you know everything; you know that I love you."

"Feed my sheep," Jesus said. "Truly I tell you, when you were younger, you would tie your belt and walk wherever you wanted. But when you grow old, you will stretch out your hands and someone else will tie you and carry you where you don't want to go." He said this to indicate by what kind of death Peter would glorify God. After saying this, he told him, "Follow me."

So Peter turned around and saw the disciple Jesus loved following them, the one who had leaned back against Jesus at the supper and asked, "Lord, who is the one that's going to betray you?" When Peter saw him, he said to Jesus, "Lord, what about him?"

"If I want him to remain until I come," Jesus answered, "what is that to you? As for you, follow me."

So this rumor spread to the brothers and sisters that this disciple would not die. Yet Jesus did not tell him that he would not die, but, "If I want him to remain until I come, what is that to you?"

This is the disciple who testifies to these things and who wrote them down. We know that his testimony is true.

The Great Commission

The eleven disciples traveled to Galilee, to the mountain where Jesus had directed them. When they saw him, they worshiped, but some doubted. Jesus came near and said to them, "All authority has been given to me in heaven and on earth. Go, therefore, and make disciples of all nations, baptizing them in the name of the Father and of the Son and of the Holy Spirit, teaching them to observe everything I have commanded you. And remember, I am with you always, to the end of the age."

Later he appeared to the Eleven themselves as they were reclining at the table. Then he said to them, "Go into all the world and preach the gospel to all creation. Whoever believes and is baptized will be saved, but whoever does not believe will be condemned. And these signs will accompany those who believe: In my name they will drive out demons; they will speak in new tongues; they will pick up snakes; if they should drink anything deadly, it will not harm them; they will lay hands on the sick, and they will get well."

The Ascension of Jesus

Then he led them out to the vicinity of Bethany, and lifting up his hands he blessed them. And while he was blessing them, he left them and was carried up into heaven and sat down at the right hand of God. After worshiping him, they returned to Jerusalem with great joy. And they were continually in the temple praising God. And they went out and preached everywhere, while the Lord worked with them and confirmed the word by the accompanying signs.

Epilogue

Jesus performed many other signs in the presence of his disciples that are not written in this book. If every one of them were written down, I suppose not even the world itself could contain the books that would be written.

But these are written so that you may believe that Jesus is the Messiah, the Son of God, and that by believing you may have life in his name.

Scripture Index

Day Three

The Wise Men Visit—Matthew 2:1–12

Escape to Egypt—Matthew 2:13–18

Return to Nazareth—Matthew 2:19–23; Luke 2:39

The Early Years of Jesus—Luke 2:40–52

The Ministry of John the Baptist—Matthew 3:1–12; Mark 1:2–8; Luke 3:1–18

The Baptism of Jesus—Matthew 3:13–17; Mark 1:9–11; Luke 3:21–23

Day Four

The Wilderness Temptation of Jesus— Matthew 4:1–11; Mark 1:12–13; Luke 4:1–13

Who Is John the Baptist?—John 1:19–28

John Identifies Jesus as the Son of God—John 1:29–34

The First Followers of Jesus—John 1:35–51

The Wedding at Cana—John 2:1–12

Jesus at the Temple—John 2:13–22

Early Reaction to the Miracles of Jesus—John 2:23–25

Day Five

Nicodemus Meets Jesus—John 3:1–21

John the Baptist Points to Jesus—John 3:22–36

Parables of Weeds, Seeds, and Leaven—
Matthew 13:24–43; Mark 4:26–34

Parables of Treasure, a Pearl, and Fish Nets—
Matthew 13:44–53

Day Thirteen

Calming the Storm—Matthew 8:18, 23–27;
Mark 4:35–41; Luke 8:22–25

Casting Out Demons—Matthew 8:28–34;
Mark 5:1–20; Luke 8:26–39

Healing the Sick, the Blind, and the Possessed—
Matthew 9:18–34; Mark 5:21–43; Luke 8:40–56

A Final Visit to His Hometown—Matthew 13:54–58;
Mark 6:1–6a

Day Fourteen

Workers for the Harvest—Matthew 9:35–11:1;
Mark 6:6b–13; Luke 9:1–6

The Death of John the Baptist—Matthew 14:1–12;
Mark 6:14–29; Luke 9:7–9

An Attempt to Rest—Matthew 14:13–14;
Mark 6:30–34; Luke 9:10–11; John 6:1–3

Jesus Prophesies His Death and Resurrection—
Matthew 16:21–23; Mark 8:31–33; Luke 9:22

Take Up Your Cross—Matthew 16:24–28;
Mark 8:34–9:1; Luke 9:23–27

The Transfiguration of Jesus—Matthew 17:1–13;
Mark 9:2–13; Luke 9:28–36

Healing a Demonized Boy—Matthew 17:14–21;
Mark 9:14–29; Luke 9:37–43a

Day Eighteen

Predicting His Death—Matthew 17:22–23;
Mark 9:30–32; Luke 9:43b–45

Who Pays the Temple Tax?—Matthew 17:24–27

Who Is the Greatest?—Matthew 18:1–14;
Mark 9:33–50; Luke 9:46–50

Restoring Broken Relationships—Matthew 18:15–20

Forgiveness without Limit—Matthew 18:21–35

Journey through Samaria—Luke 9:51–56

The Cost of Following Jesus—Matthew 8:19–22;
Luke 9:57–62

Day Nineteen

Jesus Arrives at the Festival and Begins Teaching—
John 7:10–36

Parable of the Ten Minas—Luke 19:11–27

Mary Anoints Jesus for Burial—Matthew 26:6–13;
Mark 14:3–9; John 11:55–12:11

Day Twenty-Nine

The Triumphal Entry—Matthew 21:1–11, 14–17;
Mark 11:1–11; Luke 19:28–44; John 12:12–19

Cursing of the Fig Tree—Matthew 21:18–19;
Mark 11:12–14

Jesus Cleanses the Temple—Matthew 21:12–13;
Mark 11:15–18; Luke 19:45–48

Greeks Want to See Jesus—John 12:20–36

Isaiah's Prophecies Fulfilled—John 12:37–50

Day Thirty

Lessons from the Withered Fig Tree—
Matthew 21:20–22; Mark 11:19–26; Luke 21:37–38

Jesus' Authority Challenged by the Sanhedrin—
Matthew 21:23–27; Mark 11:27–33; Luke 20:1–8

Parable of the Two Sons—Matthew 21:28–32

Parable of the Vineyard—Matthew 21:33–46;
Mark 12:1–12; Luke 20:9–19

Parable of the Wedding Banquet—Matthew 22:1–14

Day Thirty-Three

Judgment When the Son of Man Comes—
Matthew 25:31–46

Betrayal Begins—Matthew 26:1–5, 14–16;
Mark 14:1–2, 10–11; Luke 22:1–6

Passover Preparation—Matthew 26:17–20;
Mark 14:12–17; Luke 22: 7–16

The Dispute over Greatness—Luke 22:24–30

Jesus Washes the Disciples' Feet—John 13:1–20

Someone Will Betray Me—Matthew 26:21–25;
Mark 14:18–21; Luke 22:21–23; John 13:21–35

Day Thirty-Four

A Terrible Prediction—Matthew 26:31–35;
Mark 14:27–31; Luke 22:31–38; John 13:36–38

The Last Supper—Matthew 26:26–29; Mark 14:22–25;
Luke 22:17–20

Don't Let Your Heart Be Troubled—John 14:1–14

If You Love Me—John 14:15–31

Remain in My Love—John 15:1–17

Day Thirty-Five

Expect Opposition—John 15:18–16:4

The Spirit of Truth—John 16:5–15

Day Thirty-Seven

Trial—Roman Phase One (Pilate)—Matthew 27:2, 11–14; Mark 15:1–5; Luke 23:1–5; John 18:28–38

Trial—Roman Phase Two (Herod Antipas)—Luke 23:6–12

Trial—Roman Phase Three (Pilate)—Matthew 27:15–30; Mark 15:6–19; Luke 23:13–25; John 18:39–19:16

The Road to Golgotha—Matthew 27:31–34; Mark 15:20–23; Luke 23:26–33a; John 19:17

Day Thirty-Eight

Jesus Is Crucified—Matthew 27:35–44; Mark 15:24–32; Luke 23:33b–44a; John 19:18–27

It Is Finished—Matthew 27:45–50; Mark 15:33–37; Luke 23:44b–45a, 46; John 19:28–30

Supernatural Events—Matthew 27:51–56; Mark 15:38–41; Luke 23:45b, 47–49

The Death of Jesus Confirmed—John 19:31–37

The Burial of Jesus—Matthew 27:57–61; Mark 15:42–47; Luke 23:50–56; John 19:38–42

The Tomb Is Sealed—Matthew 27:62–66

Day Thirty-Nine

The Empty Tomb—Matthew 28:1–8; Mark 16:1–8;
Luke 24:1–8; John 20:1–2

Peter and John See the Empty Tomb—Luke 24:12;
John 20:3–10

Jesus Appears to Mary Magdalene—Mark 16:9–11;
John 20:11–18

Jesus Appears to the Other Women—
Matthew 28:9–10; Luke 24:9–11

The Soldiers Report to the Jewish Authorities—
Matthew 28:11–15

Appearance on the Road to Emmaus—Mark 16:12–13;
Luke 24:13–35

Day Forty

Appearance in the Upper Room—Luke 24:36–49;
John 20:19–23

Thomas Sees and Believes—John 20:24–29

Appearance to Disciples by the Sea—John 21:1–24

The Great Commission—Matthew 28:16–20;
Mark 16:14–18

The Ascension of Jesus—Mark 16:19–20;
Luke 24:50–53

Epilogue—John 20:30–31; 21:25

About the Authors

Steve Laube has been in book publishing for over forty years as a bookseller, editor, publisher, and literary agent. He serves as a Bible teacher and is married with three daughters and two grandsons. He is a Hall-of-Fame honoree of Grand Canyon University's College of Theology.

Amanda Jenkins is the lead creator for *The Chosen*'s extra content. **Dallas Jenkins** is the creator of *The Chosen*. They live with their four children in Texas, where *The Chosen* is filmed.

About the Christian Standard Bible

The Christian Standard Bible aims to draw readers into a deeper, more meaningful relationship with God. By translating Scripture into the clearest possible modern English, the CSB allows readers to experience God's Word at its fullest.

Developed by one hundred scholars from seventeen denominations, the Christian Standard Bible faithfully and accurately captures the Bible's original meaning without compromising readability.

The CSB was created using Optimal Equivalence, a translation philosophy that balances linguistic precision to the original languages with readability in contemporary English. In the many places throughout Scripture where a word-for-word rendering is clearly understandable, a literal translation is used. When a word-for-word rendering might obscure the meaning for a modern audience, a more dynamic translation is used. This process assures that both the words and thoughts contained in the original text are conveyed as accurately as possible for today's readers.

The CSB provides a highly accurate text for sermon preparation and serious study, translated from the biblical languages by scholars who love God's Word. Yet it doesn't compromise readability and clarity for those who may be less familiar with the traditional (and sometimes difficult) vocabulary retained in some translations. Research shows the CSB is both highly literal to the original languages and highly readable, achieving an optimal balance of the two.

Pastors and laypeople can read and share the Christian Standard Bible with confidence, knowing the truth of God's Word will be communicated effectively.

For more information, visit CSBible.com

Resources

Harmonies of the Gospels

Daniel, Orville E. *A Harmony of the Four Gospels: The New International Version*. 2nd ed. Grand Rapids: Baker Books, 1996.

Knight, George W. *A Simplified Harmony of the Gospels*. Nashville: Broadman & Holman, 2001.

Pentecost, J. Dwight. *A Harmony of the Words and Works of Jesus Christ*. Grand Rapids: Zondervan Publishing House, 1981.

Thomas, Robert L., and Stanley N. Gundry. *The NIV Harmony of the Gospels: New International Version*. New York: HarperCollins Publishers, 1988.

Chronological Bibles

Chronological Life Application Study Bible: New Living Translation (NLT). Wheaton, IL: Tyndale House Publishers, 2012.

The Chronological Study Bible: New King James Version (NKJV). Nashville: Thomas Nelson Publishers, 2008.

Guthrie, George H. *Reading God's Story: A Chronological Reading Bible*. Nashville: Broadman & Holman, 2011.

Smith, F. LaGard. *The Daily Bible: In Chronological Order*. Eugene, OR: Harvest House Publishers, 1984.

Blended Gospel Harmonies

Boettner, Loaraine. *A Harmony of the Gospels*. Phillipsburg, NJ: Presbyterian and Reformed Publishing, 1976. [A new edition of the same book originally published in 1933.]

Cheney, Johnston M., and Stanley Ellisen. *The Greatest Story: A Unique Blending of the Four Gospels.* Sisters, OR: Multnomah Books, 1994. [A revised version of *The Life of Christ in Stereo* published by Western Seminary in 1969.]

Dimitrov, Nikola. *The Four in One Gospel of Jesus Chronologically Integrated According to Matthew, Mark, Luke, and John.* 2nd ed. Ventura, CA: Nordskog Publishing, 2017.

MacArthur, John. *One Perfect Life: The Complete Story of the Lord Jesus.* Nashville: Thomas Nelson Publishing, 2012.

Simmons, Brian. *The Life of Jesus: Harmonized Gospels Reader's Edition.* The Passion Translation. Savage, MN: BroadStreet Publishing, 2018.